Lucky Star

Beryl Buck Miller

Big Band Singer

Television Star

Golf Professional

The threads of our life experiences weave together to form the Tapestry of who and what we become.

"LUCKY STAR" is Beryl Miller's second book. Her previous book was a Golf Instructional book and collection of her golf columns, "The Happy Golfer", titled "PLAY A ROUND WITH BERYL MILLER" published in 1980 by Arnott Publishing Co. of Stamford, CT.

Proceeds from Lucky Star will be donated to the LPGA fund for The Susan G. Komen Breast Cancer Foundation.

Copyright 2007© Beryl Miller and Arnott Publishing Co.
International Standard Book Number
978-1-4276-2217-4

Cover and book design by Curry Printing, Hilton Head Island, SC
Published in the United States of America by
Data Reproductions Corporation

Preface

So many times I have heard "you ought to write a book". So now in the years 2006 and 2007 I have undertaken this project and here it is for your pleasure.

Thanks go to my family for supporting me with the idea to write this book. Also, thanks to Ian Harries who was of great help with my computer technologies, and to Kaye Black for her many suggestions and ideas.

Foreword

I first met Beryl Buck Miller in the early 1960s at Harder Hall Golf Resort in Sebring, Florida, where her husband, George, was the golf professional. Beryl was an amateur golfer then, having enjoyed a successful career as a big band singer. Later on, she turned pro and taught in one of our Arnold Palmer golf facilities.

Beryl's recollections of the people she met – from her Canadian roots to her later life as a singer, TV personality and golf pro – remind us that life is to be lived to the fullest and that, more often than not, we make our own luck.

I applaud her support of the LPGA's Susan G. Komen Cancer Fund and wish her the very best.

Arnold Palmer

Nineteen Twenty-Four

When I was two and a half years old, my father decided to move his family from Regina, Saskatchewan Canada to Weslaco, Texas located on the Rio Grande.

My Dad's younger brother, Carl, had just bought a ranch there and wanted to convince his brother to move down there too. My Dad had two younger brothers, Carl and Stanley. They were all graduates of the University of Saskatchewan. My Dad's father died when he was about nine years old and so the three boys most surely were involved with responsibilities at the family farm.

My widowed grandmother lived in Regina and owned a huge ranch, or farm as they called them in Canada. It was a section of land, 6000 acres, and she supervised the running of the whole place. I guess it was too much for all of them, for even though Carl had made the move first, it wasn't too many years before they had all left Regina. Grandma Clara was a most independent lady and very talented, She was a fine artist and a taxidermist. She had many great adventures in her life and she later moved to Vancouver and built a great home. She had a special room with all glass doors where many of her precious birds were on display.

In her later years she would travel to Florida for the winter and was interviewed by the local Vancouver Paper as one of the first people to fly coast to coast in the 1930s. She said "It was fine but the noise of the propellers was pretty hard to take for nine hours." She also took a cruise through the Panama Canal, which was pretty adventurous for a widowed lady in the thirties. All of my life I was inspired to take a cruise through the Panama Canal and finally, some 75 years later, we took a family cruise to South America and on into the Panama Canal. What a wonderful experience! Thanks to my great Grandmother for the inspiration.

1924

So here we were on our way to Texas - my Dad, my Mom, my older sister Lorena and me. I was two and a half years old and my sister was five. When we crossed the Canadian / U.S. Border, the officer in charge asked if we had this and that and any firearms. My Dad said no and my sister piped up and said, "What about that gun you use to shoot rabbits." My Dad handed it over and he was pretty mad at Lorena because it was an heirloom and had belonged to his father. Well, we were on our way and no turning back. In a day or two it started getting warmer and my Dad put the top down on the car. A little further down the road my sister pulled my Teddy-Bear from me and threw it out the back of the car. I started to cry and by the time my Mom realized what had happened we were too far along to turn back. Ah me, I was very sad. However I have never lost my love for a handsome Teddy-Bear.

We arrived in Weslaco, Texas which is on the Rio Grande and the border of Mexico. It was very hot and we all felt it after coming from cool Regina, Sask. In a short time I came down with a case of malaria. I recall having many bad dreams and one about the GREEN DEVIL, which was a recurring dream. Also a dream I named "Big and Little" where everything was enormous or tiny. Guess it was all due to high fevers. I recovered and a few months later I came down with a second case of malaria. The doctor said, "This child cannot live in this climate." So my parents started thinking about a move back north. There were a few incidents at this time that made a lasting impression on me.

One day my mother drove across the Mexican border to a neighboring town to see a live Bull Fight in a big arena. It was exactly like the ones you see in the movies, and so was the fight. Well, that wasn't too bad. Another day she drove into the town of Weslaco to see the movie "The Hunchback of Notre Dame" with Lon Chaney. It was the big hit movie of the twenties. Well, I can recall being scared to death, and in fact being upset that my Mom would want to see such a scary movie. Some 40 years later when we lived in Sebring, Florida in the winter months, I took my boys to the local Saturday matinee many times and when the movie was the least bit scary, all of the kids in the movie that we knew would come and sit all around us. There were no other parents there and it was funny to see all of the kids gathered in a big bunch in the center of the Theatre.

One thing I do recall enjoying, but my mother forbade me to go, was the native women where the families were housed out back of the main Ranch House where we lived. They used to make corn cakes that they patted between their hands and then roasted on a fire. I would run down and get a corn cake and boy did I love them.

One day when we were returning from a trip to town and my mother was driving, there was a lot of screaming going on in the back seat and it wasn't until my mother drove up and parked in front of the house that she realized that all of that screaming wasn't just fun. There was a rickety bridge over a canal at the entrance to the ranch and the glass window in the rear of the car had hit me on the head and broke. There I was with blood running down my face and pieces of glass sticking in the top of my head. Back to the doctor again!

Before too long, we packed up everything in the Model T and headed northwest, ending up in Spokane, Washington. We lived there for the better part of a year before moving on.

My sister and I were constantly singing duets and I can remember that as if it was last year. We were guests at the local church one Sunday. We sang "Jesus Wants Me For a Sunbeam" and "What a Friend I Have in Jesus". The congregation loved us and it was great fun. And so the seeds of my future singing career were sown.

1926

Again it was time for us to hit the road and we traveled on up and crossed the border again to arrive in Vancouver, B.C. Canada. My Dad was looking for a business and this future shining city was already pretty big and busy and so beautifully designed and built. I was about four and a half years old and staying at home with my Mom. My sister had started school and I couldn't wait.

I was born in Indian Head, Saskatchewan, a University town north of Regina. For some unknown reason, I got the idea that because I was born in Indian Head I had Indian blood in me and so, at the very tender age of four or five, I started telling people that I was a half-breed. This information came back to my mother and she was very annoyed at me for saying such a thing. Of course it implied that my father was an Indian. Where do kids come up with such unrealistic ideas?

Another significant incident happened to me at this time. One night as I lay in bed ready to sleep a vision appeared at the foot of my bed. A beautiful tall, white angel appeared, larger than life and said to me, "I will take care of you." The next morning I couldn't wait to tell my mother about my vision. She said, "that's nice" but I believed in my vision and always felt protected, all of my life.

1927

I started school and loved it right off the bat. Now that I was in school life became more interesting. We also started piano lessons when I was six and my sister was nine. I was always in some school play or whatever and it was like water off a duck's back.

1929

In 1929 my younger sister Shirley was born. As she grew up I took care of her a lot, and she was a doll. In her teen years she started studying the Harp, A very complicated instrument. She gradually developed into a fine concert harpist. She played with the Vancouver Symphony and a few years later when my family moved to California, she played with the Inglewood Symphony. While still in Vancouver, she played on a weekly CBC Network radio show in 1949 that featured me and a Jazz Quintet. It was really good music. A couple of years later when I was living in New York and singing at NBC I had a very similar show, but no harp.

Shirley wtih Vancouver Symphony - 1949

BERYL, CLAYTON, DOT, LORENA, SHIRLEY 1934

49th and YEW ST. VANCOUVER. 1932
BODEN GIRLS.

GRANDMA BODENS' GARDEN. 1934.
VANCOUVER, CANADA.
LORENA, SHIRLEY, DOLORES, BERYL.

1930

The school system in Canada was outstanding and I truly loved learning everything I could. I was very interested in sports and was a good runner. One day when they held a sports or field day, I was entered in any number of events. My specialty was the 100 yard dash and they had this one event where all of the contestants took off their shoes and threw them in a great big pile. We started the race, ran 100 yards to the pile of shoes, found our shoes and ran back to the starting line. I got there first and so far ahead of the second place runner that the race officials conferred and decided to run the race a second time. Now this was a race for boys and girls. So no matter how I felt, they ran the race a second time and I won again! They gave me the blue ribbon, but I have not forgotten that incident and I guess that was when the seeds of my sports career were planted.

My father's love of automobiles blossomed into a successful business. Soon my parents were building their dream house in the Kerrisdale, Shaughnessy outskirts of Vancouver. I really loved this house and one or two others in my life I'll tell you about later.

1933

In grade six, the school decided to start a band and any students who were interested had to beg, borrow or buy an instrument. My Mom and I went downtown to the music store and looked at several instruments and settled on a B Flat soprano saxophone. The same instrument used by Kenny G. It's the most alto saxophone and is a lot like a heavy duty clarinet. It has a beautiful mellow sound as you would know if you have listened to records by Kenny G. And incidentally, Kenny is a fine golfer, as are many musicians, something to do with rhythm no doubt.

Well the band would meet once a week in a classroom and believe me, the music was not good. Remember the movie "The Music Man" with Robert Preston and Shirley Jones? Well we never got as good as the very first time Shirley Jones actually got the band together for a practice. I guess that most of those kids left their instruments in the case and forgot about it but I liked the instrument so much that I kept practicing. However, the piano was still my instrument and I continued to take lessons and practice dutifully. Where my B Flat sax ended up I'll never know. Many years later I bought a Steinway Grand and was the second owner. That piano is now 100 years old and plays so beautifully. What a tone!

In that very same year our home room teacher recognized a talented girl in our class who had the ability to tell terrific stories off the cuff. Her name was Pat Taylor. She would get up in front of the class and mesmerize the class with an adventurous story. She was so good and I remember after school a friend would meet with her in her chauffeured limousine and off they would go. Not too long after, her friend got her driving license and she gave up the limo driver. Her name was also Pat Taylor, and I'll fill you in on some surprising details about her later on.

As I was becoming a teenager, I had the joy of living in a great home with a great family and lots of music in our home. By the time I was fourteen and in high school, my running days were over. My body had filled out and I was aware of the boys looking at me. To this day I don't wear tight clothes. All of the kids at school were pretty conservative, nothing like today! High school was great and there were so many subjects and fields to learn. I was an A student and not prone to any hi-jinks. My father was very stern and none of his girls would ever go against his orders. But he did love his family so much. A couple of years earlier when I was in junior high school, he arrived just as school was being dismissed for the day to pick me up in a huge black limosine that was used for the parade of the visiting King and Queen of England. After their trip was concluded the limo was up for sale and my Dad was taking a test drive. He wanted the height of luxury but my Mother said NO!

1935

Back in 1935 I started taking popular piano lessons. I loved the jazz and rhythm of this new to me music. I had previously received a piano degree from the Royal Conservatory of Music from Toronto so I had a pretty good background in classical music. After a few months of this kind of piano playing, the teacher asked me to appear on his weekly radio program. I remember that I played "12th Street Rag", FAST! Then the announcer gave me a brief interview. He asked me what I wanted to do with my music as I grew up. I was fourteen at that time. I said I wanted to be a singer. After the show, my mother who was waiting outside the studio for me said "I didn't know you wanted to be a singer." "I didn't know that either", I said, "it just came out and surprised me too."

I loved Glen Miller and his big band and singer Ray Eberle for one. The threads of my life tapestry were again at work forming their work of art. I am reminded of Karen Carpenter who, with her brother, formed their duo and made many hit recordings in the sixties and seventies. She played the drums and he played multi keyboards. They were into a recording session and concerned about needing a singer. Karen piped up "I can do the singing." So she did a number and they were all amazed at how talented and terrific she was and no one had really known.

She was such a fine singer, one of the all time greats and she sadly died in her thirties so we lost her fine talent too young

All of the homes in Vancouver had basements and were usually built to be playrooms or family rooms. We had a huge recreational room with a player piano that we used for parties. In our living room we had a beautiful grand piano, so I was always at one piano or the other as were others in our family. My mother was a classical singer and belonged to a group that often came to our home for little concerts. My sister and I still sang lots of duets and also played a lot of piano duets. We were always invited to all of the parties. They always asked us to play. One day I said to my sister, "What if we didn't play the piano, do you think we would get invited to so many parties?"

1936 - 1939

I was often involved in activities in high school. One year a friend of mine, June Culbertson, and I decided that the school should have a cheerleading team at the big interhigh track meets. So we practiced some cheers, put on some cute clothes and went to the track meet at another part of town. There were three of us and we would get up from time to time and go into one of our little routines. It was a lot of fun for us, but no one else seemed to pick up on this idea and it died! Also during this time I recall being part of a big jump rope display at a huge interschool event. There must have been about fifty of us all doing the same routine individually at the same time. It was pretty complicated and we all loved doing it. It was hard work and I only wish I could do some of those routines now. HA! One other event is prominent in my mind, a large dancing group. Again about thirty girls volunteered and we learned a pretty tricky routine. The school made costumes for us and the sleeves had a large piece of fabric hanging down so when we raised our arms we were supposed to look like airplane wings. We practiced a lot and should have had no mistakes during our actual performance. We crossed alternately at one point in the dance and one girl crossed at the wrong time and ran into me full speed. I remember trying to hold up my arms and yet I wanted to fall down. No one else seemed to really notice and the show went very well.

1940

I sang in school concerts and my singing took over my piano playing. After high school graduation, I kept busy with many things, and in the beginning of 1940 I happened to see an advertisement in the daily paper where Doug Raymond's Big Band was looking for a singer to start with their opening season date, Valentine's Day and requested that only experienced singers need apply. You were to write to a newspaper box. Well, I wrote the letter and said that I was not experienced and also "You wouldn't want to discourage a diamond in the rough, would you?"

They called and I went in for my first audition. I GOT THE JOB! Doug later told me that the phrase about the Diamond in the Rough really intrigued him. They played three nights a week at HAPPYLAND, a dance ballroom on the grounds of the Pacific National Exhibition and Amusement Park. It was a long way from where we lived and as I did not yet drive I had to take the interurban train those nights to get there. Then I had to return the same way after one AM. But I just loved it and being with all of the fine musicians that made up the band. One time the band came to our house for a rehearsal because there wasn't any other place available at that time. What a lot of fun it was learning the Big Band business. This band was about fourteen pieces, as were most of the bands. Some bands were even eighteen and twenty pieces and more. The men all wore tuxes and the singers were always elaborately dressed in evening gowns. So I started on February the 14th and it was wonderful. I learned a lot with my first Big Band. How to sing a song with such a big background, when to come in, and where to go with a song.

In April, just barely two months after starting with Doug Raymond's Band, I received a phone call at home from a tenor sax player with another band and his name was Stan. He was helping line up singers with another Big Band. He asked if I would be interested in auditioning for the singing job with Mart Kenney's Band. This was amazing as Mart Kenney was the Tommy Dorsey or Glen Miller of Canada. They were currently playing at the Panorama Roof of the Magnificent Vancouver Hotel in the heart of town. Their singer Georgia Dey wanted to retire after five years. They usually toured across Canada in the spring and fall.

This Great Hotel is still superior to most hotels as are all CNR and CPR in Canada and was built in the 1930s to honor the first and only visit of King George and Queen Mary of England. I remember their visit and parade through the main streets of Vancouver when I was sixteen or seventeen. CNR stands for Canadian National Railway and CPR stands for Canadian Pacific Railway.

So I agreed to attend an audition at the Panorama Roof and my mother drove me into town. Because at eighteen I did not drive I was told that one of the musicians was heard to say, "Jeez, they're coming with their mothers now"... Well I guess that there were a lot of girls auditioning for the job and in fact there were two or three others ahead of me and so I had to wait. Well, I sang "Billy" and something else and then I waited and enjoyed the beautiful surroundings and opulence of this magnificent hotel. The Old Vancouver Hotel had been in the next block and when I was about eight years old my grandmother took me there one night for a rare concert in the big ballroom. On the stage was a twelve foot grand piano and when Paderewski entered with his white shock of hair it was very exciting. When he sat down to play the audience was enthralled. I will never forget that concert.

Well, I got the job, lucky me, and had to say goodbye to Doug Raymond and his band at Happyland. He said to me "I knew you were too good to be true!" A very nice compliment.

The Mart Kenney band was finishing up their engagement in Vancouver and preparing to go on tour across the country. First I went with them by one of the Princess boats across the inlet, a seven or eight hour trip to Victoria. Once again I was bowled over by this great and beautiful huge hotel, The Empress. Many, many years later I would visit the hotel on a stopover from a cruise to Alaska. I was equally impressed the second time, even though I had been many wonderful places around the world.

I did not sing yet and simply sat all night listening and watching the performance of the band. It was the farewell performance for singer Georgia Dey, who was retiring. The music was so good. This band was the Tommy Dorsey of Canada and was run like a well-oiled machine. Fifteen or sixteen men and a singer. It was awesome to watch! Back to Vancouver where they played one more job prior to going on tour. One last time in the Great Ballroom of the Vancouver Hotel. This time I was the singer! I wore a white chiffon dress. Someone had sent me a corsage of flowers to wear and when I sang my first song I was shaking so badly that the flowers were trembling. Seems so long ago. There was another singer with the band, Art Hallman. He played alto sax and when he sang he came forward to the mike and sang. He was a terrific singer and very popular with the crowd. Also, there were two others guys that came forward when we became a quartet. This kind of arrangement with a quartet was very popular in the forties and fifties with the big bands in Canada and USA. Well my debut went very well and Mart was pleased.

In a few days I'm at the railroad station with everyone else preparing to board our car and leave for the summer. It was May. My mother, as usual, had brought me and my luggage to the station and my boyfriend also came. He was a great guy, Bob Bennett. He was a gymnast and had come to Vancouver with his family from the USA. He was a sweetheart and very handsome. So I boarded the train and sadly I never saw Bob again.

The band traveled in their own private railroad car, First Class. They were a lot older than I and very kind. Two or three of their wives traveled with them. It was extremely well organized.

Our first stop was in Calgary where our car was parked on a sidetrack. We motored by bus to the hotel where again we played in the big ballroom. The show was a sell-out. This was only my second time to sing with the band and this time I was not so nervous. It was just great and it was beginning to sink in how super lucky I was. Next morning we were at the railroad station waiting to be hooked up and there were a bunch of kids at the station waiting to get our autographs. A first for me, and such fun.

We traveled across Canada, always the same plan. There were always huge crowds at every performance. A lot like present day rock concerts. The impressive hotels we played at were always a delight. One about as good as the next. For the rest of my life I would desire to stay at or at least see the great hotels wherever I traveled.

On one trip in Ontario, several of the guys in the Band took a side trip to see the Dionne Quintuplets. And I also went to see them. They lived in a special facility in Calendar, Ontario. They had a special playtime when visitors could see them. They could not see us. They had constructed an outdoor play area that was screened in and they all came out at once, dressed up in darling dresses and on tricycles, all riding around the track on the outside of the playground. Those five girls

Regina, Sask.
Sunday, June 2/40
By Don McLeod.

really led a very sad life separated from their family and constantly on display to make money for their support.

After about four weeks of touring, we arrived at the railroad station in Banff Springs. The town was so delightfully charming with its wide Main Street that led up to the huge hotel about a mile up to the foot of a mountain. One of many. The surrounding mountains were beautiful and some were still snow-capped. If I was taken with all of the hotels where we had played, I was over-whelmed at the sight of the Banff Springs Hotel. Like a great castle in the clouds. This was my all time favorite and still is more than sixty years later. In the eighties, Werner and I took a long trip across Canada which ended in Banff. I was again overcome with the magnificent natural beauty and the man-made beauty of the hotel. This trip, we played golf wherever we stopped. The Golf Pro at Banff welcomed us and said I was the first LPGA member to play there. The next day we had a gallery trailing us as we played!

Back to the summer of 1940. One day again several guys invited me to go along to a beautiful natural setting as well as yet another fabulous

Man-Made Monument, the Lake Louise Hotel. Again on that Canadian trip in the eighties, we went to see Lake Louise. Even better, we drove up the Mountain Highway to Jasper. A fine destination with its own super golf course. We played and had the same experience as at Banff. The Golf Pro said I was the first LPGA member he had ever had play there. We played with a fine golfer from California. At the time we were there Princess Margaret, Queen Elizabeth's sister, was visiting. It seemed there was a very casual security which reminded me of a trip one time to Texas where President Jerry Ford was speaking at the Sweetwater Country Club, in Sugarland, Texas. At that time, the LPGA was headquartered there. A National Seminar was in progress for the LPGA. Another gal and I cut out of a meeting for a break and actually we were anxious to see Jerry Ford. He always was very fond of the Professional Lady Golfers. He was giving a speech in another large meeting room and we were able to crawl right in front of him and take pictures. However, there were a lot of men milling around and I was assured that they had run checks of everybody at the club. Obviously these men who seemed to just be hanging around were the F.B.I. and we were members of the LPGA who were also at the Sweetwater Country Club for a national seminar and tournament.

We had a special instructional seminar by Teaching Professional Hank Haney who moved on to become Tiger Woods' instructor. He was great and it was most informative. Patty Berg was there as well as Peggy Kirk Bell and Gloria Armstrong. Gloria played in my foursome and I don't recall how well we did as a team but we did play pretty well.

Back to the summer of 1940! I was learning my singing business pretty well and certainly enjoying the Big Band Business.

One night young Mickey Rooney sat in with the band and played drums. He was so dynamic and energetic and fun to watch. Famous forties debutante Brenda Frazier Duff was there with her entourage, and in general the guests were a quality group. Another outstanding guest was actor Henry Fonda and his family. I don't recall if Jane and her brother Peter were with them, but they were a delightful group that stayed for about two weeks. Banff was an elegant destination in the forties and there were many activities. Golf, Tennis, Swimming - indoors and out. And horseback riding, which was my favorite in those days. I rode about three times every week and when my parents came to visit, they also went riding one day. Another day, I walked along with my parents while they played golf as I had done before in Vancouver and in Harrison Hot Springs, a fine resort in British Columbia, east of Vancouver. So this day in Banff, my Dad wanted to convince me that I should take up golf, and on a par three with an elevated tee he wanted me to hit a ball. Of course I had played a lot of tennis, but I said to him, "I don't even know how to hold the club." Now I was left-handed and so was my Dad, so he shows me how to hold the golf club and I take a couple of swings and put the ball in the middle of the green. "See, you're a natural" he said. So, when they left he left his golf clubs with me to go and take a lesson from the Banff Hotel Golf Pro. The Pro asked if they were my clubs and then advised me not to start learning left-handed. He said that it was very difficult to get ladies left-handed clubs and also he felt that I would be a better golfer if I learned to play right-handed. So I thanked him and didn't think about golf again until I returned to Vancouver in September.

Nearly forty years later on a trans-Canada trip my husband Werner and I stopped at Banff. It was just as awesome and we had a wonderful visit at the Hotel, the Hot Springs and the golf course. When we signed up to play, the Golf Pro said I was the first LPGA Member to ever play there. When we later went up to Jasper Lodge, the Pro there said the same thing. I guess I should have told him that forty years earlier I had sung there with a Big Band.

Well the summer of 1940 rolled on and I loved it all. We practiced every morning and had the afternoons to do with as we pleased. Many of the guys in the band played golf. I went swimming or horseback riding or whatever. I had a seamstress in town make me a couple of very nice evening gowns and did some shopping in the unusual shops in town. Before long the fall plans all started to fall into place. The band was making a major move to Toronto. I was still eighteen and didn't even want to think about such a move, so after some concerts on the road, I returned to Vancouver. I had loved the summer, but it was really good to be home.

Alan Young was the star of a new comedy and musical show on CBC (Canadian Broadcasting Company) and they were conducting auditions for a girl singer. So I went to the audition and got the job. Lucky me! I was now nineteen years old. This was a national network show and Alan was very popular and indeed he deserved to be.

Harry Price was the conductor of a 25-piece orchestra, a studio Big Band. What a treat that was! I also did some little acting bits in the skits that Alan had written for the hour long show. They were very funny and no doubt that Alan had a great future. He also could play the Bagpipes and would write a bit into the show utilizing that talent. One day Alan invited me up to his apartment to run through some skits. He was a perfect gentleman and I was too naïve to pick up on any advances. Years later when I met up with Alan in New York, I was considerably more experienced and I understood a play when I saw it.

This show ran for only a few months as Alan was getting good offers to go to Hollywood. He starred in several movies but his big hit was the TV Show "Mr. Ed". With the talking horse. It ran for years. I met Alan again many years later in Westport when he was making an appearance as a lecturer. I went up after the lecture and spoke to him and he was of course delighted to see an old Show Business friend. However it was the fall of 1970 and I was soon to be married and so that was it. I never saw him again, but have many good memories. Another outstanding talent in Vancouver at that time was a fine actor named Fletcher Markel. He appeared on many drama shows. He seemed to be part of the CBS crowd and I enjoyed his personality. He also left Vancouver in that era to join the ORSON WELLES drama group that was just blossoming.

One of the most spectacular clubs in Vancouver was the Cave Supper Club. It was built to create the impression that you were entering into a giant cave. The walls and ceilings were all dark gray and craggy with the effect of stalagmites and stalactites all over. There was a large elevated stage and Earl Hill and his Big Band played there nightly for dancing and floorshows featuring entertainers from New York and other big cities. Mostly American acts. I approached the owner and arranged to have an audition with the band and once again, I GOT THE JOB! Lucky me. It was a good job and once again I enjoyed singing with a big band. Over the years even when I no longer worked there, I enjoyed this club and met many big-time stars. Lena Horne was my favorite. Martha Raye was insanely funny and she traveled with her husband, one of the Conti Brothers. Both of those entertainers came to my home for a party that was simply great. Then there was Sammy Davis, Jr. who first appeared as the Will Mastin Trio starring Sammy Davis, Jr. There was a little after hours club that we all often went to and Sammy would go there too. We all told him, on the side of course, that he needed to make the break and go solo. Well he did eventually and became one of show businesses biggest international stars. When Frankie Lane sang "Mule Train" it brought the house down. I recently saw Frankie singing on a fund-raiser on public television and he sang "That's My Desire". He is now 90 years old. Terrific!

1941

In the spring of this year, I decided to try my hand at making an arrangement for the band. I selected "Am I Blue?" and spent some time getting it all done. It was more complicated than I had anticipated. You write a master score for the entire band and then you copy off the individual sheets for each instrument. Now a copyist must know his music because you can copy some of the parts, but others have to be transposed into another key. Brass and reeds go up a tone or a third while the percussion instruments stay in the same basic key. Piano may have a fistful of notes, bass has one note and the guitar may simply use popular music chords. So when I finished, I brought it for the band to play. It was a big deal for me and I was disappointed in how it sounded. Too simple! But I learned a lot and it would come in useful in the future.

Also in the spring of this year I had a rather strange visit. Mart Kenney was in town and came to the Cave Supper Club to watch the entertainment, hear the band and me. Afterwards he invited me to come and visit him in his room at the Vancouver Hotel. I thought he had a paternal interest in me and we talked about Banff and the band now in Toronto and so on.

So he says, "Well, how about it?" I said, "How about what?" He says, "I want you to go to bed with me!" I said, "Are you kidding? I'm a nineteen year old Virgin and proud of it." Then I left! I never ever saw him again! Another lesson in life about men! However, back in those days it was the norm for girls to save themselves for marriage.

One of my big songs to sing was the Dinah Shore hit "Blues in the Night." One Sunday evening the entire band went to a big military base outside of the town limits. There was an exceptionally large auditorium where we were to perform. The band set up and played a couple of opening numbers and then it was my turn. I came out in an attractive evening gown and when the band started to play the introduction to "Blues in the Night" there was such a monstrous roar from the audience that I was stunned. I was almost blown over and at first didn't know what all the commotion was. Think of the Bob Hope military shows . . . this was the same thing. The war in Europe was in progress and these military shows were often the last thing that our servicemen got to enjoy before being sent overseas to fight. I never forgot that experience!

I sang at the Cave for nearly a year and had become friends with many of the musicians in Vancouver. I had started dating Dal Richards whose big band played at the Panorama Roof atop the Vancouver Hotel. The same room where I had auditioned for Mart Kenney's Band before their move to Toronto. This Hotel ranked number one on my all time list of favorites forever. So beautifully designed and constructed for the Canadian trip the King and Queen of England took to Vancouver in 1937.

After hours on the job at the Cave, I would walk a half block to the Vancouver Hotel and wait for Dal who would drive me home. We lived in the same part of town. His band singer was Juliette, an outstanding new young star who later became a fine television performer in Toronto. Her sister Suzanne also was a fine singer and I was quite friendly with both of them. Many years later when I was living in Manhattan, they both came to New York for a visit and we went out a few places. It was great fun reminiscing about our early days in Vancouver.

On December 7, 1941, the Japanese bombed Pearl Harbor. It was such a dastardly deed and the whole world was stunned. Living on the coast of the Pacific Ocean our Canadian government took immediate steps to protect our coastline. The west coast was put on a Blackout Law. All cars and vehicles had to drive at night with their lights shaded. All nighttime lighting was either turned off or put on low wattage and shielded. Homes had to install blackout drapes on windows and doors. Indeed we all felt threatened by the Japanese after the attack on Hawaii and those conditions existed for about one and a half years or more. My Dad had given me a car to drive, which helped a lot because my hours at the Cave were often different from Dal's Big Bands' hours.

My car was a big HUPMOBILE, probably a 1936 or so model. A good looking car and very solid. My mom had given me driving lessons and soon I was good to go.

In the Pacific Northwest, you must learn to drive with foglights and in the fall and winter it can get pretty foggy. As recently as the summer of 2005 on our annual trip to the mountains in Maine, we took Route 81 through the mountains on our way to Albany and we ran into very heavy fog. I was driving and it was very strange because I felt as though I was driving in Vancouver again, some sixty years ago. Another thread in the tapestry.

1942

Dal Richards was certainly one of Canada's top Band Leaders and had a great deal of knowledge about the Music Business. He started in the Kitsalino Boy's Band in Vancouver. They were mostly around sixteen years old and were internationally famous. They traveled across Canada and also took a trip to Europe. So Dal had been in Paris as a teen-ager. He tells a story of how he was determined to bring home a loaf of French bread. He got some lacquer and painted the bread and carried it everywhere the band went trying to preserve it. Not too far

DOWN BEAT

CHICAGO, APRIL 1, 1943 Vol. 10—No. 7

Triple Threat

Vancouver, Canada—They call lovely Beryl Bodenne a triple threat girl, because she sings, plays second piano and arranges for the Dal Richards band. Speaking of threes, she and the band are rounding out their third consecutive year on the Panorama Roof of the Hotel Vancouver.

from coming home, it broke in half and he chucked it in the garbage. E for effort.

Dal played reeds, alto sax and clarinet, and he formed his own band while still in Magee High School. I remember that band on stage of the auditorium when I was in grade ten. Dal took first year college at Magee and then left to start a most successful career. He also had a very good singing voice a la Ray Eberle, who was probably the most popular male singer of that era.

1943

I was quite content with my singing job with Earl Hill and his Big Band and enjoying all of the Floor Shows at the club. At this time, the government decided that they would levy an entertainment tax at any facility that had floorshows and featured entertainment. The Cave was a perfect example. They came to Dal and said that if his Band's musicians played that was fine, but a girl singer fell under the category of entertainment. So Juliette had to go. Don't feel sorry for her because she soon moved to Toronto and became a big time hit back east. In a few years when television became the hit program, she had her own network show. Anyhow, Dal came to me and asked me to join his band as a pianist who also sang. There were two grand pianos on the stage, just waiting for a second pianist. So I said goodbye to the Cave and joined the Dal Richards Big Band. It was great and certainly the top job in the country. Now I had to join the MUSICIAN'S UNION . . . 802 which was headquartered in New York City.

Dal had a knack for publicity, and when gas became rationed in World War II, he hired a horse and buggy that posed in front of the Vancouver Hotel for the daily paper and it represented the new era of Gas Rationing.

The Panorama Roof was such a popular place and we had celebrities of every ilk attending every night and no wonder. The food was served and often prepared table-side. The staff was largely European and extremely well trained. For me it was my first encounter with the proper way to serve caviar. And of course our music. As good as any big band and full of unusual ideas. We had two grand pianos on the stage, one on each end. It was a beautiful set-up. One feature that was fun and interesting to the audience was different musicians swapping places in some numbers. I would switch over to first piano and the pianist would go and play drums, and the drummer, who was also multi-talented, would play a trombone solo.

One night Eddie Cantor and his wife Ida and their family came for dinner. Another night Baron Rothchild and his entourage came for dinner. In fact he came several times. Bob Crosby and his executive director Perry Botkin came a few times and in later years they continued their friendship with Dal. So, I knew Bob Crosby well enough to look him up a few years later when I lived in New York and he was playing with his orchestra at the Strand Theatre.

The Mills Brothers had a long engagement at the Palomar supper club across the street from the Vancouver Hotel. We went to hear them a few times. They were wonderful. We also got to know them pretty well. One night one of them came to the Panorama Roof for dinner and to hear the band. He brought his lovely wife and we enjoyed seeing them. Also another night we were invited to an after-hours party at someone's very big home. I played the piano for Don Mills to sing and he loved it! Being a singer, I knew just exactly how to accompany him. I saw Don Mills again many years later when I was on a trip to Las Vegas for a golf tournament. He remembered me and that night my friend and I went to see their great show.

1944

Probably our most famous visitor was Howard Hughes and his date, Yvonne DeCarlo. Yvonne was originally from Penticton, British Columbia. They sat at a table for two and I doubt that too many people bothered them. They were pretty much lost in the shuffle of a most sophisticated crowd. As it happens, possibly they were there because Yvonne wanted to see the Roof and also Dal had taken her out one time. She was already quite successful in Hollywood. We often would go over to a table to say hello to visitors and so I went over and said hello. Howard was very, very quiet, but it was my pleasure to meet him. My Mother was up there that night gathering information for a newspaper column she wrote weekly for the local paper, a Who's Who column, so she went over and got a short interview.

Strangely enough my family had connections with Howard Hughes. My father's youngest brother Carl Boden, lived in Inglewood, California, and worked for the studios that Howard owned, where they filmed Jane Russell in her first movie, "The Outlaw". Howard was working on his massive plane "Hercules". Howard was very fond of Carl and one day he said "Hey Carl, you want to go for a ride? I'm taking up Hercules for a test run over Long Beach Harbor." So, Carl went and he was one of only about 9 or 10 men who had that privilege. In fact he sat in the co-pilot's seat. Hercules never flew again and was eventually moved to a town outside of Seattle where it sits today, a museum piece. The press nicknamed his plane the "Spruce-Goose".... a name that hung on and Howard hated it.

In the fifties, Howard Hughes lived in Las Vegas, and my sister Lorena was an executive secretary at Summa Corp., which was Howard's company. He was a brilliant man who helped our military personnel with many suggestions in World War II. And incidentally he was a single digit handicap golfer whose favorite golfing buddy was Kathryn Hepburn.

It was a most glamorous life and we were always busy, busy. Very soon, Dal and I became engaged and started to build a house. As I look back, I don't know how we found the time, but busy people always get things done. We did a lot of the work ourselves and finally we were coming down the home-stretch. We started to make our plans for our wedding.

"Musically Yours"...
Dal Richards,
Beryl Bodenne
and all the boys.

Panorama Roof   Hotel Vancouver

1945

The Ryerson Church was a United Church of Canada. In Canada, the Presbyterian, Methodist and Baptist churches joined together to form the United Church. This church was a magnificent building and catered to many weddings. I had a lot of personal ties to this church.

My parents were not church goers and how they were involved in that Baptist Church in Spokane where my sister and I first sang as little kids, I'll never know.

In 1945 we lived about four blocks from the Ryerson Church and when I was about ten years old, I started going to Sunday School all by myself. At Christmas in 1932 I wanted my own Bible for a gift. I still have that nice little Bible. It is seventy-five years old. I went every Sunday and by the time I was sixteen or seventeen I was helping out in the Nursery Class with those darling, cute little five year olds. When I returned from my summer at Banff, I started teaching in the pre-school

Sunday School. However, as time rolled on I had to give it up due to the late hours I was keeping Saturday nights.

Years later when my two sons were three or four I started taking them to Sunday School in Westport, Connecticut and also in Sebring, Florida, where we lived for 10 winters. When they became teen-agers they went on their own sometimes. Gary often remarked to me when he was an adult and living on his own how often he remembered so much of his Sunday School teachings.

On March fifth, 1945, we were married in the Ryerson Church. It was a lovely White Wedding and we had about 150 guests. We had a super reception at one of the large banquet rooms at the Vancouver Hotel. When we opened the bar, everyone was stunned and started asking where we got all of the liquor. Liquor was rationed to one or two bottles a month per person, no exceptions. I had planned for our reception for a long time and put away my monthly ration along with a couple of others. I even took my grandmother to the liquor store to boost up my supply. We had all of the traditional showers and so on and the reception was perfect.

We stayed in a beautiful suite at the Vancouver Hotel that night and the next morning we boarded a train to San Francisco. Our biggest night there was at the Palace Hotel where Freddie Martin and his singer, second pianist Merv Griffin were playing. Merv's big hit at that time was "I've Got A Lovely Bunch of Coconuts", which was such a fun song and I had heard Gracie Fields sing this song in 1940 at the Banff Springs Hotel. I wondered if Merv had ever met Gracie Fields. She lived in London.

San Francisco was just wonderful, but we couldn't stay too long, as we were not able to leave the job at the Roof for more than a few days. It would be many years before I returned to San Francisco. Probably my most favorite city in the world is Vancouver. It is indeed a most magnificent city and a natural harbor. If you stand in the middle of the city and look across the harbor, you see Grouse Mountain which is usually snow-topped. What a scene! The forefathers who planned the city did a great job and it is only a little over a hundred years old. One of the assets that sticks in my mind is the abundance of fine beaches.

As a kid I learned to swim at Kitsilano Beach and also Spanish Wells beach. Second Beach had built a breakwater that created an outdoor pool of some size. I remember learning to swim longer distances in that pool and also spent some time learning a few dives. The one swimming experience that sticks in my mind happened in 1946. Dal and his pianist Bud Henderson would often go swimming late at night after the job. So one night we pulled up to a spot in Burrard Inlet and they decided to go for a swim across the Inlet to the other side. It was at least 800 yards. So off we went and the water was great. About one third of the way across I started thinking this is too far for me and I nearly turned back. But Bud kept egging me on and when he got to the other side he stood there and kept yelling at me to come on. He really saved my life because without his encouragement I might have quit swimming. He was one sweetheart of a guy and no one else seemed to realize that this was too far for me. When I got to shore, I was exhausted. They didn't swim back but someone went and got the car. That same big Chrysler Station Wagon that we had at that time. My other beach experience was at English Bay when modeling swim suits for Rose Marie Reid. I wonder if all of those famous beaches are still beautiful and called by the same names.

World War II was still in full progress in Europe and Japan but things were doing better for our forces overseas. London had suffered very badly from all of the bombings, but when I first traveled to Europe in 1970, there was very little evidence left. Amazing how much restoration had taken place.

The Dal Richards Band was very busy and our lifestyle consisted of rehearsals, playing the job and parties, parties, parties!

We would often go to the Cave Club to see the headline acts. We became well acquainted with some of them and had some good parties with our new friends. One activity that was very enjoyable was to attend the Vancouver Symphony performances with guest conductors. These performances were usually held Sunday nights at the Capitol Theatre.

Built around the same time as the Radio City Music Hall in New York and Grauman's Chinese Theatre in Hollywood, California. These theatres were built to last, and so they have. One of the guest conductors that came often was Sir Thomas Beecham from London. He was an imposing figure and he certainly knew his way around a Symphony. I also remember Leonard Bernstein who first came to Vancouver as a young man in his twenties. But he performed well beyond his years and was very popular. He stayed mostly in the East as he got older and was an enormous favorite with his programs for the young people. He lived in Fairfield, Connecticut, not too far from where I lived for many years.

DAL RICHARDS, BERYL BODEN AND THE BOYS

PANORAMA ROOF   HOTEL VANCOUVER

1946

The Hudson's Bay Company is a big department store in Canada and was named after the very old company that originally specialized in fur trading. Now it is the Saks of Canada. They were always on top of the latest fashions and held live fashion shows in the store two or three afternoons every week. Marie Moreau was in charge of the shows and she asked me to be a model. There were about eight girls in each show and so I agreed to try it out. It was a lot of fun and was a new professional opportunity for me.

Marie was from France and was such a charming lady and very talented. Her commentaries were always very interesting. A few months later, she decided to retire from that aspect of her life and asked me to be her successor. I agreed and found it to be a most interesting job. However, it did not take long for me to realize that it was too much and I had to quit. But another thread in my tapestry was being woven and this experience came in handy many years later.

The Dal Richards Band was growing in fame and stature and we were playing at many outside functions but still at the Panorama Roof for dinner and dancing Wednesdays, Fridays and Saturdays.

Dal became quite involved in conducting a larger band than we normally had. We would play at the Malkin Bowl in Stanley Park during the spring and summer and usually on a Sunday. Dal would add a string section for these concerts in the Park and they were very well attended. Mr. Malkin who paid for the concert Bowl was in the tea and coffee business and it was very successful. His home was another of those mansions that took up an entire city block and was fenced in with a huge brick wall. This great mansion was no more than a block from my family's home and yet I never did get to go inside those great gates.

One special party we played for was a huge private party at a very big mansion. This was probably one of the grandest and biggest homes I will ever see. Not as grand as the Biltmore Estate in Asheville but a close second. It was an entire city block in the outskirts of Vancouver and was built and owned by Austin Taylor, an entrepreneur of some renown. He was an impressive figure of a man. Tall, and large framed with a full head of silvery hair. I have no idea how many children they had, but this party was for Pat Taylor, his daughter. Remember that name from my grade six days at school? Well, she had gone to New York and attended Vassar College and now had returned home only to prepare for her forthcoming wedding and her return to New York City. She married William F. Buckley and yes, she became Pat Buckley, the prominent New Yorker. A Fashion Plate and always involved in so many of the functions of the city that raised funds for charities. I was a big admirer.

Busy, busy playing at a variety of events. In the Spring of this year, Dal chartered a plane to take the entire band on a trip to Jantzen Beach Pavilion in Portland, Oregon. We were going to see the Les Brown Band of Renown and simply spend the evening mingling amongst the crowd of fans. Of course, I loved watching Doris Day on the bandstand and her hot number at that time was "Sentimental Journey". It was a quick trip, but a real treat for all of us.

There were some great Big Band singers in the business at that time. Doris Day with Les Brown, Jo Stafford with Tommy Dorsey, Helen O'Connell with the Jimmy Dorsey Band, Helen Forrest with Harry James Band and then she also went with another Big Band or two. Rosemary Clooney with Tony Pastor's Big Band. Lena Horne had first sung with Xavier Cugat, but made it into the movies right off the bat. Harry James was married to Betty Grable and she was a singer, but not a Big Band singer. Anita O'Day was also a top notch singer and one night, many years later, several of us went into New York to hear her sing a new program. She sang so great and one song, "Wave", a latin song, really caught my attention and I added it to my own program and it is still one of my all time favorites.

One weekend in the early summer there was a great regatta planned out in the Burrard Inlet and we were asked to sit and play on the top deck of a big yacht. The whole bay was filled with boats of every kind and our boat sort of drove around casually and we played and I sang over a P.A. System to entertain all of the smaller boats. I can remember singing "Sailing, sailing over the bounding main" too many times.

1947

One night we were playing a special event at another big auditorium when a lady came up to me and asked if I would be interested in being a model for pictures of some of her new swimsuit line. Her name was Rose Marie Reid and her career as a swimsuit designer was taking off big-time. So I agreed and we met a couple of days later at the English Bay Beach. She also had a good looking guy there to model men's suits and, of course, the photographer. He was very efficient and I had the pleasure of working with him again a couple of years later for a series of fashion photos. So we did the shoot and it was quite a lot of work. I don't recall getting paid very much but it was interesting and fun. She soon moved to Los Angeles and became an international fashion swimsuit name. Speaking of the photographer, he took some fine pictures of me that appeared on national entertainment covers. A few years later when I was living in New York, I did a cover for " Field and Stream", pretending I was fishing.

Later that year we had a somewhat dangerous experience that I never forgot. Dal had just purchased a beautiful new Chrysler station wagon, a "Woodie" as they were called in those days. Such a big beautiful car! One night, after playing until midnight, Dal wanted to take the car for a long run and so we hit the highway and drove down to Seattle. These Pacific Coast Highways are six and eight lanes wide and straight. At that hour of night there wasn't any traffic and so Dal decided to give his big car a good test! Off we went and no exaggeration we were up to 120 miles per hour when a cop pulled us over and had us follow him into the local police station. There were three of us. Now Dal had a restricted license due to his vision and Ken, the other guy had the same license. We should have been going 55 miles per hour. We sat quite awhile, paid the fine and started back up the highway to head home to Vancouver. The police car was tailing us! The front seats in those days were one big seat and Dal says, "Here, take the Wheel", and slides over and under me. Now I'm driving the limit which is 65 miles per hour. The police car pulls up along side of us and I smile at him, somewhat sadly, he throws his hands up in the air and drives off!

What a night! What a car! But I was no daredevil and the entire incident did not sit too well with me.

1948

In the first week of January I received a phone call from New York. It was Jim Farmer of "HI, LO, JACK AND THE DAME". They had played at the Cave Supper Club about a month or two earlier and we had gotten to know them very well and spent many after show hours with them. I had even sung with them at a rehearsal at the Roof one day and I loved this kind of group singing. Well, it turned out that their Dame wanted to retire and they were offering me an opportunity to sing with them and get to visit New York City and so on. Needless to say, I was very flattered but reluctant and Dal and I discussed this situation. He was 100% in favor of my going, and I sadly had to admit that our marriage had become a show business relationship. I hustled and got my life reorganized and off I went. Dal had no trouble finding another singer and he was most anxious to have me get the experience of being in New York.

The day I was to leave in January was a very foggy day and all flights out of Vancouver were cancelled. So, I had to take a bus to Seattle and take a flight from there to New York. When the bus crossed the border, two immigration officers boarded the bus. They checked people out and asked me to follow them into an office. They asked me the same questions as they had asked on the bus and then said I could go. To this day I have no idea what that was all about unless they were just trying to amuse themselves.

Now Vancouver has a snowy and cold winter but when I arrived in New York, I was chilled like never before. The eastern seaboard gets very cold in the winter and I had to learn how to live with that. Fortunately, I had a very nice Silver Fox coat which had always been very pretty to look at, but now it was a life-saver.

I was met at the airport and whisked away to New Jersey. The quartet lived in the country farm house of their manager, Bob Brooks. His wife, Joan Brooks, was currently living in Richmond, Virginia, and was the featured soloist on a big weekly radio show. That was very much the popular thing at that time. So it was at the farm that I rehearsed with Hi, Lo and Jack and memorized their library. Hi was Maury Laws, a tenor and fine guitar player who hailed from Roanoke, Virginia. Lo was Jim Farmer, who had come to New York from Florida, and sang baritone. Jack was Jack Steinbrenner, another tenor who came from Pennsylvania. His wife was Kathy, who traveled with us wherever we went. Several years later I learned that Jack had gone to Vietnam and had been killed in the line of duty. I had lost touch with all of them over the years and I was sad to hear about Jack. He was also a good musician and did the arranging for the group.

Our manager had an apartment on 54th Street just down from the Museum of Modern Art, or MOMA as it is often called. We stayed there when we were in town and it was such a great location for everything.

We started our current singing engagements and our first show was at a theater in Philadelphia. It was very big and although the die was cast, the days of live entertainment at area theaters was winding down. However in the late forties there were a lot of theaters that still featured a stage show after every movie. Radio City Music Hall in New York City lasted with this format until the eighties or nineties.

Well it was terrific and so much fun! A lot different from singing with a band where you put your own style and interpretation to each song. Here you had to all sing exactly alike and not get carried away with your own style. We sang in perfect four-part harmony and it sounded wonderful! We sang at so many different places and when we sang at a theatre in Charlotte, North Carolina, my picture was on the front page of the Charlotte paper. Great!

In the spring of 1948 we sang at the Balsams Resort in Dixville Notch, New Hampshire. This was a long way out of New York, but was worth the trip. A very beautiful hotel with magnificent grounds and a superb golf course. I was not yet seriously into golf or I would have tried to play that course. The scenery was awesome. About 45 or 50 years later my son George, who had moved to Maine nearby, played and won a Regional Golf Tournament at the Balsams and that was also a win for me!

The BALSAMS, Dixville Notch, New Hampshire

Don't see how we can miss, now that we have Beryl! See you at the "Pent-house" — Maury
Things here are fine, and I know that Vancouver's loss is our gain. As ever, Jim.
Thanks for lending us a swell gal So Touche' from Touche' Jack 48
Dear Dal: May our continued success equal yours, All my love, Beryl.
James J. Kriegsmann N.Y.

All of the guys in the group were good musicians. Jimmy played the piano, Jack played bass, and Maury played guitar. I used to sing a lot of songs with Maury when we practiced and when our manager heard me singing "Nature Boy", a song made popular by Nat King Cole, he had us put the number in our act as a solo for me with the boys in the background. In the late fall, we took our second trip to Montreal to play at the Copacabana Club. We also did an appearance at a local theatre. We also did "Nature Boy" and it was the hit of our act. They loved it. And I received a few fan letters in response. It is still one of my all time favorite songs.

One day when we were all in New York we went backstage at the Capitol Theatre where Patti Page was the headliner. They had all worked together previously and this was my first time to meet Patti. THE SINGING RAGE, PATTI PAGE. She was a darling, so cute and tiny and friendly. And her song " How Much Is That Doggie In the Window?" was one of her big hits at that time. I recently also saw her on a Public Television special and she was great!

Hi, Lo, Jack and the Dame were to appear on a national radio show where the audience voted for their favorite. This show was for Professional Entertainers. We were told in advance that we were not to be the winners, but someone else had been pre-selected. I thought that was pretty shoddy. Years later when it came out that the quiz show "21" had been a fix, it reminded me of my experience with Hi, Lo, Jack and the Dame. What a joke! I still have the telegram that I sent to Dal about listening to the show and that we were not supposed to win! The audience loved us, but to no avail. Even in 1948 there were ethical questions.

When we were up in Montreal I had to go into the Canadian Immigration Offices and appear before a board to extend my Visa. I had done a lot of preliminary work in Vancouver in January, but it was time to work out an extension.

While we were there, a local radio station contacted me and asked me to make a tape for them to use for their Theme Song as they came on the air. It was a good experience and they also made me a couple of tapes for my own use. I understood a few years later that the D.J. played that theme song with me singing for years to come. Terrific!

Back to New York for a few days and I saw where Bob Crosby and his big band were playing at the Strand Theatre with the Clark Sisters. So I saw a great show and then went backstage to say hello to Bob. He flipped because of course he did not know I was in New York.

After the 9 PM show we went out and he took me a lot of places I had not been to previously. We went to Bill Miller's Riviera on the Jersey Coast just over the George Washington Bridge. A great club with top-of-the line food, entertainment and service. I can recall the name of the headliner, Lenny Bruce. He was a hot entertainer who had a most risqué act that brought roars from the crowd. I have never before or since heard so many four letter words rolled into one monologue. It may have been entertainment (?) but as television was just starting to get going, his kind of act never made it. He was not Milton Berle!

The next day Hi, Lo, Jack and Kathy went back to New Jersey and, with some time off, I stayed on and went a lot of places with Bob Crosby. He was a lot of fun and knew his way around the city. One night we went to the "21" restaurant and then across the street to a great Jazz Club.

Ella Fitzgerald was appearing there with a jazz quintet. What a treat! She was my favorite all time singer and still is. She came over to our table and visited for a long time. I can remember as if it was last week. How lucky can you get!

One evening Bob said "I'm taking you some place special" and off we went in a cab to Greenwich Village. We got out at a big house that was two or three stories tall and featured a bar on the main floor. The bar ran the length of the building and, as we walked past the bar to the end of the building, everyone turned and stared at us intensely. It was a Lesbian Bar and in those days they all had a dyke look that was recognizable. I was wondering what was up when we reached a flight of stairs going up we came into a wonderful apartment. It belonged to the lady who was the owner of the building. She was kind of an Italian Mama to the Crosby boys, Bing and Bob, and whenever they were in town, she cooked them a fabulous dinner. There were about ten of us for dinner and it was superb. Well, it was a great night that I never forgot! Many years later I ran across Bob Crosby at golf events and I'll get to that later on.

One weekend we went up to a big function in Holyoke, Massachusetts, and it was a one show job. I remember that area well and years later I went to Mt. Tom in the Holyoke area to ski with my two sons. I also skied with my son George many places, but most outstanding was Zermatt, Switzerland, the home of the great Matterhorn Mountain. What a good trip that was.

Back to 1948. We performed at many more theatres and I recall one in Binghamton, New York. It was a grand theatre and very carefully designed with loges and balconies so as to handle large crowds. It reminded me of the Roxy Theatre in Manhattan. It was hard to believe that they tore down the Great Roxy Theatre in the sixties to make way for yet another office building.

Of all the engagements we played I was most impressed with the Westchester Country Club just north of New York City. What a great place, really a hotel with every kind of facility you could wish for. Years later I played a tri-state golf tournament on this course. My second husband, Golf Professional George Buck, played in the PGA tournament held annually at the Westchester Country Club a few times, so I also went to watch and was part of the gallery. One night we were guests of the PGA at a dinner to honor Hale Irwin for winning the U.S. Open.

So the days and nights with Hi, Lo, Jack and the Dame rolled on. We had an outstanding engagement at the Steel Pier Theatre in Atlantic City. We were there for two weeks and in the adjoining ballroom, Tony Pastor and his Big Band were playing nightly. His singer was Rosemary Clooney. I loved the beach right there beside the Steel Pier and swam in the Atlantic Ocean many afternoons.

Later in the year we were booked to come and sing at the massive Convention Center the week after the Miss America Contest. That week we stayed in New York, and in the morning Jack discovered that someone had broken into our car and stolen the majority of our band

PLAYBILL

Hi, Lo, Jack and The Dame head the
Stage Revue at Steel Pier, Atlantic City

Page 26

WEEK OF JUNE 12, 1948

15c

arrangements. Now this was a big problem because the orchestra that was to accompany us was about thirty pieces. We got to Atlantic City early and Jack and I spent a day and a half copying new sheets for the band. Fortunately the thieves had not stolen the briefcase with the original arrangements. Right up to the minute we were to rehearse with the band, we were copying like an assembly line. We were pretty tired but we got through it all somehow and the audience loved us.

It was very educational getting to see so many different cities and one other incident in Montreal comes to mind. Late one night after the show, three or four of us went to a very late night club in the Jazz section of Montreal. One of my fiends was a fine pianist who happened to be in Montreal at the same time playing at a big hotel. It was so late and the live music was gone for the night. So my pianist and I got up on the bandstand and sang and played a half dozen songs, including some blues improvisations. A tall, handsome and well-dressed man came up to the bandstand and offered us a job to sing in his club. We smiled and said "No thanks." What a hoot!

On this trip north, we stopped in Albany for a theatre engagement. We were the opening act for Abbot and Costello. Lou Costello was so funny and when we finished our last number, "Ragtime Cowboy Joe", he ran out and started dancing with me all over the stage. The audience loved this horseplay and so did I!

However, the year was winding down and I was getting pretty tired of living out of a suitcase. That was pretty tricky because I had to carry three or four fancy gowns also. We were all getting kind of restless and talking about where we would go for Christmas. I made my decision to return to Vancouver and we all agreed to call it quits. Our Dentyne Chewing Gum commercial was a bonus worth remembering. We sang it at every single show!

DENTYNE CHEWING GUM, IT'S KEEN CHEWING GUM....BUY A PACK TODAY!

The last engagement for us was a show at CBS in New York City. We went into the studio to meet with Carl Reiner who was the writer for the show. He later was associated with the Show of Shows with Sid

meandering with music

VOCALISTS — Save on Arranging Bills. We carry complete Vocal Orchestrations in your key. Catalog Free.
DANCE BANDS — All Publishers' popular and standard Orchs. and Orchets. Lowest Prices. Catalog Free.
SHERWOOD MUSIC SERVICE
1585 Broadway, New York 19, N.Y.

We would like to add our congratulations to the many that Dal Richards and Orchestra are receiving on recently completing nine years as "The Band at the Top of the Town" playing in the Panorama Roof, Hotel Vancouver.

DAL RICHARDS ORCHESTRA
A record of some sort was achieved recently by Dal Richards and his orchestra, pictured above. Dal celebrated his ninth anniversary at the Panorama Roof of the Vancouver Hotel. Perched on the piano next to Dal (in tux), is lovely vocalist, wife Beryl. (See cover story.)

Mart Kenney opens Port Stanley on Friday, May 6th, and Crystal Beach on Saturday, May 21st. These are two of the largest dance halls in Ontario.

Len Hopkins (the man who wrote the new Canadian song hit "Sault Ste. Marie") will be moving his band from the Chateau in Ottawa to the Banff Springs Hotel for the coming season.

Paul Perry and Orchestra appear for their second year at Sylvan Lake, Alberta.

Art Hallman and his Orchestra will hold the Spotlight at Bigwin Inn for July and August.

Lew Dickson heading the Cabaneers at the New Copacabana, formerly the Village at Winnipeg.

There is some talk of Billy Duncan getting the dance job on what is known as the "Booze Cruise" to Bowen Island this year.

Alex Dawson still the popular band leader in the Standish Hall in Hull, Quebec.

The Gatineau Club has recently reopened with Harry Thompson and his Orchestra providing the music.

Johnnie Berring currently heard at The Casino will trek to Clear Lake for the summer months.

Rumor has it that Paul Grosney (our friend in Winnipeg's north end) will form a band for the Casino.

Jack Drewry will again head the band at Winnipeg Beach.

Wally Myers booked for Grand Beach on the other side of the Lake.

The Narrows Vancouver now operating six nights weekly, with Barney Potts Orchestra.

Vergil Lane, the colored flash on drums, has recently left Winnipeg on a tour of the West. The promoters have bought an old bus, and reports are that it is fixed up to really give comfort to the tired travellers. The band is known as the Clouds of Rhythm. The personell in part are as follows: Omar Williams, piano; Bill Hayes, trumpet; Vergil, on drums; Eddie, Diamond, 3rd alto. The first and second sax spots were still open at this writing. The possibility of Tony Padula, Vancouver sax man, joining the group in Edmonton was mentioned.

Bud McIntosh leader of the group at the Highwayman, is in the market for a good tenor man.

MART KENNY
Mart Kenny, Canada's number one bandleader recently celebrated his fifteenth year of broadcasting. He can be heard currently on the "Canadian Cavalcade" show, aired every Tuesday night.

INTERMISSION

Page Sixteen

Caesar. Carl was an exceptionally talented and congenial gentleman and moved on later to California where he appeared on many shows. I remember him most for his part on the Dick Van Dyke Show.

One other item of interest was being able to attend the theatre whenever I was in New York. I saw a few good shows and remember being impressed attending the Strand Theatre and seeing Sarah Vaughn singing with a Big Band. She couldn't have been more than twenty years old and she was very skinny! But she could really sing and I loved seeing her. Henny Youngman was the comedian on the bill and he was great too!

In December, I flew to Vancouver from New York and the weather wasn't too good. The plane had to land in Billings, Montana for a few hours before resuming its flight to Seattle. I arrived in Seattle to find the flight to Vancouver had left. So I finally arrive in Vancouver four or five hours late. There is a photographer at the plane with Dal to take my picture at the plane returning home.

While I was away, Dal had sold our first home and bought a larger home in a very nice area. We arrived there and found an apron, a box of cake flour, a large bowl and an egg beater. The photographer took a mock picture of me presumably making a cake. Such is Show Business! I was tired but very glad to be home even if I didn't know anything about the house.

The next night, I was singing again with the Dal Richards Band and it was all too easy. With all of my experiences in the East, I was even more appreciative of the beautiful Panorama Roof atop the Vancouver Hotel. Its wonderful architecture and superb interior design and decor were still the best I had seen.

Dal and the Band were happy to have me back on the job. One thing they had missed and we had popularized was my being able to swing around from the piano and start playing the CELESTE ad lib between numbers. A Celeste is a most pretty sounding bell-like sound with the same keyboard as the piano only smaller. It has a very pretty effect and especially when we did remote radio broadcasts from the Roof. Funny thing, many years later one of my very best all time friends in New York was a beautiful singer-actress by the name of

Celeste. We have stayed in touch and have had many wonderful times together. The very popular thing to do in those days was to have remote radio shows from the location that a live band would be playing. No one else had been able to fit the playing of the Celeste into the program that the Band played.

1949 Vancouver

Armed with my experiences with Hi, Lo, Jack and the Dame, I decided to start up a quartet of my own. I made several good arrangements and recruited three guys and we started rehearsing. We did a few engagements and one such job was at a big rally sponsored by the Kiwanis Club. We sang three or four songs and it was a big hit. However this activity gradually petered out, as we were all too busy to spend time doing this kind of singing. But I always loved quartet singing. In the U.S. the Hi-Los were my favorite and they made a lot of timeless recordings. Even forty or fifty years later they are still tops. Mel Torme and his Meltones were also very popular.

Around this time I asked Dal if I could start planning on getting pregnant and had it all figured out that I wouldn't even need more than two or three months off. He said positively no...... he did not want to have any children. After having taken care of neighbor's kids and teaching Sunday School, I was always crazy about little kids and it broke my heart to contemplate a life without any children.

We started to drift apart and it was becoming just a show business marriage. Dal was always pushing me to do this and do that. One day I drove to Seattle with our fabulous pianist, Bud Henderson for an audition at the Olympic Hotel that featured floorshow acts three or four nights a week. They liked my performance but I wasn't a big enough name for them to feature and to draw in the crowds. I realized this too, but it was a good idea. Their next featured entertainer was Hildegarde, an impressive singer pianist who was nationally known in that era.

We started going to the Cave supper Club again after hours and had a few acts back to our home for a late night party. Lena Horne was such a doll and I had a Chocolate Cake as part of the food I served. She said, "How did you know that chocolate cake is my favorite?" Well of course I didn't, but chocolate cake is my favorite, too. Lena was very impressed with our pianist Bud Henderson and tried to convince him to move to New York and accompany her, but he declined. Lucky for Dal Richards it never happened. I know she is still in New York and I am sure she is still a raving beauty as well as a lovely person.

Another great entertainer that was a favorite was Martha Raye. She had a great act and she and her husband came to our home for a party.

By the spring of 1949 I realized our marriage was over. We had been married for four years and had been so busy working, working and that was what we had. I realized the year I had spent in New York hadn't helped either although I think I thought then that it would. I didn't want to just be a professional couple and suggested that we should start our lives over while we were still young and had a chance to build a new life. Dal agreed and so we started the proceedings for a divorce. I admired him very much and respected his professionalism but the feelings I had for him had changed.

I started some correspondence with the William Morris Agency in New York. I had made some contacts there previously. They promised me some work should I return to New York.

Next, I updated my passport and all of the paperwork that was required to make a permanent move to the United States. In August of 1949 I left dear Vancouver and my family and friends and returned to New York. This time I took the train across the country with an enjoyable stop over in Chicago. I arrived in New York and checked into the Bryant Hotel on Broadway, a favorite of many entertainers. I really felt pretty depressed and lonely, and then a bouquet of flowers arrived from a friend and changed the atmosphere. I stayed there a week or so and in the interim I met Kaja Sundsten, a beautiful model from Sweden. We hit it off well and decided to share a large room at the Taft Hotel on 6th Avenue and 50th Street. We had only been there a day or two when the William Morris Agency called with a job. It was at a big club in Baltimore, similar to the clubs I was used to in Vancouver like the Cave and the Palomar. So off I went for two weeks and had a great engagement. Later I noticed a hand written note on one of my pieces of music. It said, "You really knocked me out for two weeks." He never spoke to me in person, but that was a nice gesture. This club was the Latin Quarter, Good Club, Good Band, Good Pay. When I returned to New York, I immediately went to the Chase Manhattan Bank in Rockefeller Plaza and deposited my check. A good habit that I had started in my teens. Nowadays I deposit some royalty checks from ASCAP etc..

1948

While I was in Baltimore a local radio station that was just starting up with Television programs, came to the club and asked if I would be interested in appearing on one of their local Television programs. I said "Yes," and went and did the program one evening. It was my very first TV show. It was interesting to learn to sing to the little red light when the TV camera that was shooting came on. The general public had no idea how big a part of life Television would become in the future lives of everyone. Back in New York, the big shows were Howdy Doody, with host Bob, for kids. Captain Kangaroo, again for the kids. The Show of Shows with Sid Caesar, Imogene Cocoa, Don Knotts, and Carl Reiner. It was a weekly variety show with the most impossibly funny skits imaginable. Sid Caesar would do fractured accents in every kind of locale, French, German, Italian, Chinese, you name it. The Milton Berle Show was a riot as was "I've Got a Secret" with Garry Moore. And the next year he did a Variety show with the new star, Carol Burnette. In those pioneer days there were often mistakes made. This was in the days before taping and all shows were live. Also the networks went off the air late at night and sometimes earlier. Television stations were popping up all over town and not all of them were good, so you had to be careful not to get exposed to the public on some show that was going down the tube

Kaja Sundsten had moved to California where she later married the fine actor, Burgess Meredith. He had many fine movies to his credit and later would become most famous for his role as Sylvester Stallone's trainer in the Rocky movies. Now I found a women's-only hotel on the WestSide and moved there for a couple of weeks.

On Broadway Miss Liberty was a hit show, starring Eddie Albert as a song and dance man. NBC was planning a five-morning a week show on radio starring Eddie Albert. An agent sent me to NBC Studios for an audition for this show soon to start. It was September. NBC Studios are very impressive. An escalator from the main floor takes you to the floor where you wish to go. I found out which studio and arrived to find no one there, so I sat down at the piano and started to write up a sheet for the songs I knew in case I had to accompany myself. In came two men. One was a piano player and the other was the director of the show. I was to sing the two songs they had picked, "I Love New York In June" or "How About You?" and something else. As it happened I knew those songs. So I sang them and waited outside. They came out and told me I GOT THE JOB! I was later told that they had been auditioning for weeks and had auditioned over 300 girls. Not exactly surprising considering how many people live in greater New York.

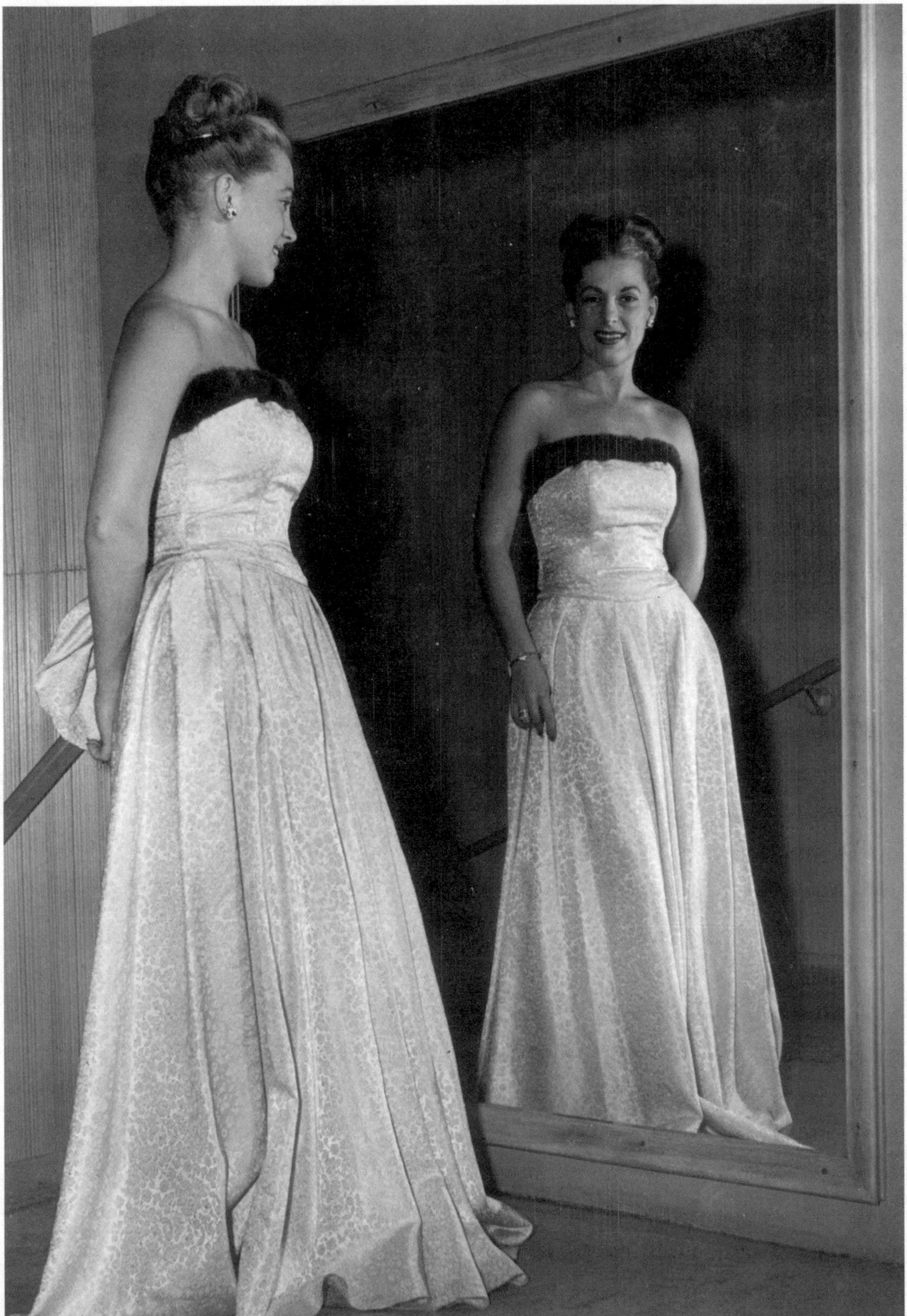

Well again, Lucky Me! I am reminded of a story about golf master Gary Player. He was practicing his sand wedge shots one day for which he is famous and a young gentleman was standing on the side watching him. As he practiced some of his shots got closer to the hole and a couple of them went in the hole. His fan says, "Golly Mr. Player are you Lucky, and that one that just went in the hole was really lucky!". "Funny thing", Gary says, "The more I practice, the Luckier I get!"

The Eddie Albert Show was every week-day morning. We rehearsed that day's show at 7 AM, took a fast break and went on the air live at 9 to 10 AM, took a break and then rehearsed the next day's show until 11:30 or 12 noon. A few times we had to rehearse in studio 6A, the great big studio where "Saturday Night Live" comes from every week for so many years now. I remember that big clock that sits at the edge of the audience. The studio we used was on a lower floor and more than enough for our morning show. In 1949, the rest of the day was mine to do whatever I needed to do. I started a ballet class at 1 PM three days a week and really enjoyed those classes. I had always loved to dance and at other times in my life I took tap dancing classes much to my delight. Many years later in Westport, Connecticut I again took some tap-dancing classes and slightly got to know Joanne Woodward, who was always taking ballet classes. These dance classes were held at the Bambi Lynn and Joe DeJesus dance school. It was very successful and popular too. A few years later, I took a series of Latin Dance classes and always enjoyed dancing with Joe DeJesus, who was an outstanding dancer. Joanne Woodward and Paul Newman live in Westport and it was not unusual to run across him in one place or another. One time I was picking up something in a little grocery store and behind me waiting to pay was Paul Newman. Those blazing blue eyes of his knocked me out!

When a few years later I wrote my first book, we tried to get him to write a foreword, but he declined. He is known for not even giving out autographs, but I do have a framed letter from him and so I do have his autograph. My foreword was written by Dick Siderowf, an all time great amateur golfer with many titles to his credit who lived in Westport.

Back to 1949 and the Eddie Albert Show! I used two alarm clocks to get up and going in the morning as I have never been an early riser. There was a trio that played the music on Eddie's new show. Johnny Smith on guitar was a pretty well known musician nationally, Arlo on the keyboards and organ, and Mort Lindsay on piano. A few years later Mort Lindsay became the conductor for the Merv Griffin Show from California and has had a very successful career.

Eddie sure did love to sing and we often did duets. I have some old tapes from those shows and they are worth keeping. Eddie's lovely wife was the great actress Margo! Her most famous role was in the movie "Winterset" with Ronald Coleman. She was quite pregnant when the show started and it didn't seem too long before she gave birth to Edward Albert, Jr. who also became a top notch actor when he became an adult. Margo did not have a long life but Eddie did and lived to be ninety-eight when he died in 2005. I still cherish a beautiful little leather jewelry box they gave me at Christmas, 1949.

I moved to a terrific new apartment and had to start buying furniture and everything else. This large house was owned by Mrs. Fender, a lovely widowed lady who took great pride in her home. The house on 73rd off Riverside Ave. had belonged to Bernard Baruch. The main floor had an enormous glass and iron door into the lobby. A doctor and his family lived on the entire main floor. His offices were elsewhere. Then a curving staircase took you to the second floor. There was also an elevator. The entire front of the house was an old library and a closet had been made into a kitchenette. It was a huge room with high ornate ceilings and an oversized fireplace at one end. There were French doors that opened out onto a balcony. This apartment was simply the cream on the cake that I was enjoying by living in Manhattan. Such a busy and exciting time for me. I started to do a lot of Television shows and my weekdays were crammed with all kinds of activities.

One incident sticks out that made me pretty annoyed. Before I left Vancouver, good friends had given me the name of a top director that they knew at CBS. They begged me to look him up and see if he could help me professionally. Well, one day I made an appointment to see him and I arrived on time to be ushered into a large, fancy office with tall windows overlooking Madison Avenue. After a relatively short conversation he said. "I will send you to any auditions I know of, but no guarantees. You have to produce what they are looking for. In exchange, you will sleep with me!" What a riot! I said, "Definitely, NO THANKS! I know I have enough talent to do it on my own." Then he tried to make it up to me by inviting me to lunch. But again, I said no thanks and I never saw him again! I did see his name on a few shows from time to time but it was really of no interest to me. End of story.

1949 New York

NBC offered me a twice weekly afternoon network radio show with the same trio that played on the Eddie Albert Show. Those little fifteen-minute shows were pretty popular with the networks at that time. Over at CBS Tony Bennett was doing the same thing. This was a delightful little show of easy listening and in that era, there was so much good music around. Cole Porter was in his heyday on Broadway and there were lots and lots of musicals in the movies as well as on Broadway. I loved doing this little show, as well as Eddie Albert's morning show, and was trying to fit in any TV offers I received. Just this year, Tony Bennett celebrated his 80th birthday and they had a spectacular special on NBC with lots of others honoring him. There was Barbra Streisand, Elton John, Stevie Wonder and two or three other singers. The staging and dancing was outstanding. So if Tony Bennett is five years younger than I am, he must have been 22 or 23 when he had that fifteen-minute show at CBS and I was 27 or 28 over at NBC Studios at Rockefeller Center. So many years ago. Today as I am writing this, the eightieth Macy's Thanksgiving parade is in progress and someone said in a newspaper article that they should have a parade float for Tony Bennett.

Sometime during this year, I had an interesting singing engagement at the "Blue Angel", a very elegant and special little club on the upper East Side. They regularly featured top-notch performers and the upper-crust especially enjoyed this club. My favorite club at that time was The

Stork Club, also on the East Side. A favorite with the smart set in Manhattan.

1950

The Eddie Albert Show had a fine announcer, Jack Arthur. He asked me to audition for some French Speaking Tapes that he was involved with. He could not understand how I came from Canada and did not speak French. The people who speak French are largely from the province of Quebec, which certainly is a large area about the size of Texas. The Canadians in the rest of the country, and definitely those on the West Coast, did not speak French. British Columbia was more of a lifestyle like California. Well, I had some high school French and so I went with him to the audition thinking I could read the script okay. But they wanted off the cuff conversational French and I was very limited in that area. But that experience was so typical of New York. Lots of action going on all the time

One time I was invited to audition for a commercial for Ford Motor Company.

'YOU CAN BUY MORE BUT
YOU CAN'T BUY
BETTER THAN A FORD.'

But Rosemary Clooney got that job. I had met her when I was singing with Hi, Lo, Jack and the Dame. Her manager, Joe Shribman, had an office in the R.K.O. Building, a tall, busy, busy place next to Radio City Music Hall. The manager for Hi, Lo, Jack and the Dame was Bob Kerr and he shared the office with Joe Shribman. Right across the hall was Jose Ferrar's office and one day I saw Rosemary and Jose coming down the hall and we all got in the same elevator. They were obviously pretty wrapped up with each other. They were soon married, moved to California and had a large family. Great talents, both of them.

I was getting to know New York City quite well and my mother flew out from Vancouver to visit me for a couple of weeks. We had a grand time and she loved, loved New York.

She would come to the Eddie Albert Radio Show in the morning and then after the show, when we rehearsed the next day's show, she would go off on her own and explore the city. Then we would meet later and go other places. I was dating a successful attorney at that time that I had met through friends the previous year when I was singing with Hi, Lo, Jack and the Dame. This couple was running the summer camp at the Balsams Hotel in Dixville Notch, New Hampshire. Today that resort still flourishes and I got to visit there with my family in 2003. A great place and so beautifully laid out with magnificent gardens. As it happened, my son George who is a professional golfer, won a tournament there in 2001. I never played that golf course, but George tells me it is a beauty!

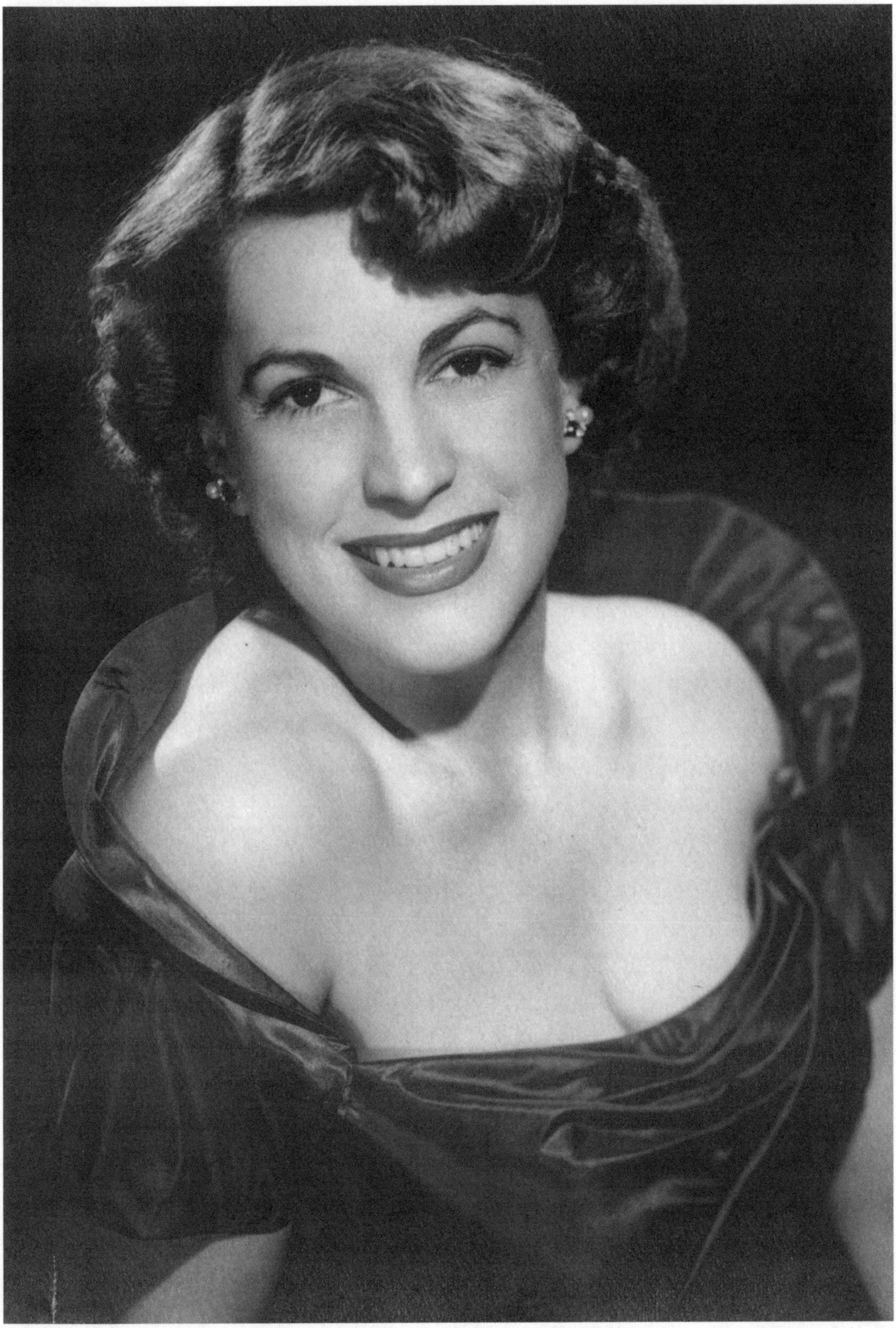

So back to the early part of 1950, my new friend came into the city and took my mother and me out to some fancy places for dinner. My mother really liked him, but it was not to be. He was very bossy and too possessive for me. A very nice guy for someone else.

Over the years I have had many recurring dreams about that era and my beautiful New York apartment. The story was that this beautiful house had originally belonged to Bernard Baruch, the international financier. Just a few blocks away they were starting to build the massive Lincoln Center as it stands today. A great art and music center.

Many mansions were built on Riverside Drive in the early part of the 20th century. Many of those beautifully designed and built houses still exist today as beautiful as ever.

I bought a piano for my apartment, and Bob Merrill, the popular songwriter, came over a few times to use it. He used to write his music on a little xylophone. Bob wrote a lot of hits in the fifties. "If I Knew You Were Coming I Would Have Baked A Cake" was one. And I believe that a few years later he was involved with the music of a Broadway Show. You meet so many talented people and then lose contact. Interestingly enough, I did not own a television set. I was so busy and always on the go, I would never have had time to watch it. There is a lot to be said about working in Television and National Radio. It is much more like running a business compared to other aspects of Show Business. I have never known any fellow performers to be involved in drugs or even excessive use of alcohol. Most of us were always prepared for our performance, on time and ready to go. A good life, actually.

In the Spring of 1950, the Broadway Show "Miss Liberty" was winding down and soon closed.

Eddie and Margo and their new baby Edward were planning to move back to Los Angeles, and also the show was going west. As it happened my fifteen minute show was also winding down. I kept that theme song as one of my all time favorites, "My Romance".

This was the end of a delightful era but my Television era was booming. Vincent Lopez and his very big band that played at the Taft Hotel nightly was starting a nice personable talk show on Dumont Television. I believe that Dumont later merged with ABC. His show was short and sweet. He was interested in my Canadian Band experiences and we talked about all of that. At the end of the show, he gave me a watch….no money! He had me on again and gave me another watch. I sent it to my sister Lorena, who was living in California.

As it happened, after Dal and I were divorced, I kept the surname Richards and it was easier for people to remember. To this day people cannot seem to get Beryl right, although it is a pretty common name in England and Canada. I had two friends in school called Beryl.

I read where Alan Young was appearing at a local theatre with a live show, so naturally I looked him up. He was so very happy to see me as he didn't know I was in New York. We spent sometime going places and it was simply great to be with someone from Vancouver who was doing so well in the movies and television. I saw him again many years later in Westport, Connecticut when he was appearing doing a lecture for some company. Again he was happy to see me but we did not go anywhere as I was about to get married again.

My next show was with the Bobby Hackett Orchestra (or Band) at the ABC Studios on 66th Street off Broadway. It was actually not too far from my new apartment on 73rd Street and I often walked home after the show. It was Thursday evenings and was a STUMP THE BAND format, probably the original show of that caliber. Somewhere in the early fifties a show did come on that was called STUMP THE BAND. They had amateur contestants and believe it or not one of the original contestants on that show was JOHNNY MATHIS.

Our format was for people to phone in or send a letter and the band would see if they knew the song. I don't recall if there was any prize other than knowing they had stumped us but also I don't recall that we were hardly ever stumped. They had a big tumbler of cards and letters and the announcer Warren Hull would pull out a letter and announce it to the band. There were two great looking gals at a table that handled the phone calls and they took turns. Sometimes I would draw the letter or card but my job was to sit on a table with a beautiful big Basset

Hound named Morgan that everyone loved. He belonged to the director of the show. We would play and I would sing some song and then we would draw the letter to see if we were stumped. I'll never forget "Blueberry Hill" was drawn and no one in the band knew it, but I did! How, I'll never know, but my brain was jammed full of all kinds of music including R & B and a great deal of Classic Music from attending many concerts in Vancouver.

"Here's Morgan" was the name of the show, and the dog belonged to Dick Richards. One evening after the show, Dick asked if I would like to drive back to Greenwich, Connecticut where he lived with his family. I enjoyed the chance to see Greenwich which has countless magnificent homes. I slept in a guest room and in the morning I met his two children. We were preparing to leave for the city when it became apparent that Morgan was missing. So we wasted most of the day looking for him and finally he was found. My current friend, Mr. S., had a "fit". I have to assume that he did not trust me! He missed the beat there because it was just a friendly little trip. Later Mr. S. was very proud of himself because he called the Greenwich Sheriff's Dept. and asked if they had found the dog. After all MORGAN was a celebrity. Needless to say I was not impressed with my friend's attitude.

That show was the last show that I auditioned for. Now someone would just call me and ask me to do this or that show.

It is amazing to remember how may Big Bands I have seen in person. In Vancouver, Big Bands were always coming to town. Nat King Cole and his band, Count Basie and his band, Lionel Hampton, Sunny Dunham, Glen Gray, Jack Teagarden, Duke Ellington to name a few. In New York, Big Bands played at the Hotels and the Astor Hotel was very big on live entertainment. I saw Cab Calloway and his Big Band and Carmen Caballero at the Astor. Also I dated Vic Damone and he stayed at the Astor. He has always been my most favorite singer and years later he came to Hilton Head Island and did a wonderful show at the Hyatt Hotel. After the show I went with my husband Werner and we had a chat with Vic. I reminded him of our dating in New York and he was very gracious about recalling. He was married to Diahann Carroll, a very successful singer-actress.

I did the Ed Sullivan Show with Ray Block and his twenty-five piece orchestra and also the Robert Q. Lewis Show with again Ray Block's Orchestra. On that show, famous jazz trumpet player Bunny Berrigan was to do a solo number, and during rehearsal the director kept moving him around so much that Bunny stopped playing and said "I can't do it your way anymore." They got it settled for the show but those young directors were mostly such know it alls that rehearsals could be a pain. I remember that I sang "The Lady Is A Tramp".

I started a series of shows called THE ARTHUR MURRAY PARTY with Bobby Sherwood and his big band. He was a very talented leader and of all his hits I remember "CELERY STALKS AT MIDNIGHT". Cute. The format was dancing and music. The show opened with about twelve couples dancing the Viennese Waltz. It was a most lovely program. One night during rehearsal the director flicked on his mike and said, "Stop talking, Beryl." I was jut sitting there but he knew me from "Here's Morgan" and I guess he couldn't tell Arthur Murray or Bobby Sherwood to stop talking and he didn't know anyone else's name.

Many years later in Connecticut it turned out that a good golfing friend of mine had been one of the original dancers on the Arthur Murray Party. Her name was Jeanne and she married a good friend of mine, Ralph Johnson, who was an avid golfer and worked part time at an Arnold Palmer Golf facility where I also worked teaching Golf. They now live in Sarasota, Florida.

The Arthur Murray Party at ABC Studios ran for a few months. It was a big hit and a pleasure to be part of. Bobby Sherwood was a great band leader and full of ideas. He negotiated a late night Television show at CBS called "Midnight Snack". It came on at 11:10 after a ten-minute news update. He asked me to be his co-host and I was delighted to do so. It was a fifty-minute show with guests and music. We would start the show in an informal setting, much like the "Tonight Show". We did not have a live audience for that show. Everything else I had done including the Eddie Albert Show had a live audience. So this was different. Bobby was very talented. His main instrument was the trumpet, but he also played piano and guitar. We would do a number or two and then have a live guest. Naturally one of our guests was Arthur Murray and his lovely wife Katherine. Arthur brought me a gift, a lovely silk scarf with Arthur Murray printed all over the fabric. I still have that scarf. So we would talk at great length with our guests and then do another number. We moved our location two or three times and my favorite was a studio upstairs in Grand Central Station. I had started to play golf again in the early spring and joined a club in Westport, Connecticut. I would take the train up for the week-end and get as much golf in as time allowed. So when we started doing the show from Grand Central Studios, Bobby allowed me to leave the studio at ten minutes before midnight and I would run down and catch the 12 AM train to Westport. I don't guess I did that every Friday, but a few times. I was taking golf lessons from George Buck, the Golf Pro at Longshore Country Club and I really loved it.

Our late night show ran opposite "Broadway Open House" over at NBC. This show was the forerunner to the Jack Paar Show. After Jack retired, Steve Allen took over and did the show for many years before Johnny Carson took over. That great entertainer ran the Tonight Show for more than 25 years before he retired. Now the host is Jay Leno.

Another popular show at CBS was with Mike Wallace and his wife Buff Cobb. It was a conversational fifteen-minute show called Mike and Buff. He is a few years older than I but I am sure that he remembers all of those early fifties programs.

A current show that is popular is "The View" with Barbara Walters and newcomer Rosie O'Donnell. Rosie O'Donnell didn't last too long die to her aggravating comments. There was a show in 1950 that starred Faye Emerson and Dorothy Killgallen, and I think Arlene Frances, similar to the present show with Barbara Walters. It was very popular and ran for a long time.

Television was bursting alive and there were tons of new ideas and shows. Just like today, some of them were hits and some didn't last more than a few times. The Ed Sullivan Show ran for many years and in the beginning it was called "The Talk of the Town" as was his newspaper column. He gave me a nice credit in his column and called me the Dinah Shore of Canada.

Over at ABC there was a weekly show with Paul Whiteman and his 35-piece orchestra. That and a show featuring two great pianists "Edie and Rack" were also on my agenda. I do remember singing "I Cover The Waterfront", a very popular song of the day.

Another show where I was asked to be a guest was the Eddie Condon Show. He was an all time great BANJO artist. It was a musical show with a Big Band and guest artists. It was a great pleasure for me and I certainly did enjoy the fine musicians of that era. These were the pioneer days of television and everyone, everywhere was busy with performances and rehearsals.

The producer for the Arthur Murray Party asked me to do him a favor. He had two friends coming to New York for a visit and they wanted to take in some of the hot clubs and would I go with them, as they did not want to go without a lady friend. So I met them and it was Alan Alda, Sr. and Jack Carson who was very popular with a big hit radio show. We went to several clubs and I remember they particularly wanted to go to THE CAIRO to hear a new outstanding comedian. His name was Jonathan Winters and he was absolutely hilarious! It was a great evening and they were perfect gentlemen, no monkey-business.

It was interesting for me when I had to join some professional organizations. With Hi, Lo, Jack and the Dame, I had to join AGVA, American Guild of Variety Artists. When I started on the Eddie Albert Show, I had to join AFRTA, AMERICAN Federation of Radio and Television Artists. Many years later I joined ASCAP, American Society of Composers and Publishers. More on that later. And of course, I remained a member of the Musician's Union for some time. One thing that was a little difficult during this busy time of so many television shows was my wardrobe. I have always liked nice clothes and had quite a lot of outfits, but not enough. I don't recall how this came about, but I started wearing dresses by Ceil Chapman, who was a very well known designer and headquartered in Manhattan. Once a week or so, I would head on down to the garment district and Ceil Chapman's offices and pick up two or three of her dresses to wear that week. It was just lovely and I was very happy to have a credit at the end of the show saying that. Also, later that year when I was to be married, they gave me a beautiful dress and jacket to wear to my wedding. Ah me, such memories.

I was getting pretty hooked on golf and went to Westport virtually every week-end. I was using a set of left-handed clubs that George loaned me and he suggested that it was time for me to buy a set of right-handed clubs, so I did!

Even though I was very tied down with Television shows and rehearsals I managed to catch the train to Westport and soak myself up with golf most weekends. My lawyer friend had taken it upon himself to try to guide my life according to his style and I was getting pretty tired of that relationship. One weekend I arrived at Longshore Country Club to find my locker completely emptied of all my stuff. Golf clubs and shoes and everything. Anna, the lady in charge of the locker-room, was nonplussed. She said "Mr. S. said you were going away and wanted all of your stuff." Well, la de da, what nerve! George heard about it and had me go to the house owned by the Vice-President of the club while I decided what to do.

Funny thing, about three or four weeks earlier Mr. S. and I were having dinner at a local restaurant on a Saturday night and George was there with a pretty lady having dinner and I noticed them. Mr. S. said, "That's his wife."

A few weeks later, I was up at the club and in the golf shop and George said to me "I'd sure like to put a ring on your finger!" I said, "That's not a nice thing to say." He said "Why not?" I said "because you're a married man." He said, "I am not, I was waiting for you!" Well what a surprise! He was indeed a most attractive man and looked a lot like Greg Norman, only better looking for sure. But I just left it at that and kept coming up for my golf lessons week-ends, while the attraction was growing on both sides. So I guess my lawyer friend was trying to block my interest in golf by taking all of my things.

Well, it didn't work! Soon George and I started dating. He would drive into New York and I would train up to Connecticut week-ends. That must have been hard for George because his hours were very early each day. He had been a captain in the U.S. Army from 1940 to 1945 in the European Theatre. His younger brother Gordon had been in the U.S. Air Force and flew many missions into France and Germany before being lost at sea. This was about the same time that Glenn Miller was also lost at sea in the same area. Such a huge loss those lives of our fine young men. George's mom was a widow and he had a lovely sister who married around that time. We were pretty friendly and a few years later, they, Mary and Tony moved to Naples, Florida and continue to live there. We stay in touch.

George loved to sing and was most interested in my singing career. I was still doing a lot of shows and only came up to Westport for week-ends. One weekend in May George finally got his wish and put a diamond ring on my finger.

Part Two

The beginning of my golf life and career

October 1950

In the fifties and sixties many club golf professionals played the "Winter Tour" which ran from November through March, and George had done just that for the winters of '47, '48 and '49 after he had returned from Europe. He had been in the U.S. Army after Pearl Harbor and retired as a Captain. He returned to Europe one year, I believe 1948, and played in the French Open. He won and was indeed most proud of himself. He wanted to play the PGA tour again in 1950, so we settled on a date to get married on October 22nd and then leave for the tour. The tour started with the North South Open in Pinehurst, North Carolina.

In the first week of October, I did my last five shows with Bobby Sherwood at CBS. Our guest on the Friday was George Buck who gave the first golf lesson on network TV. Bobby Sherwood was an avid golfer and he loved it! Soon after Bobby Sherwood moved to Las Vegas and lived there for a long time. I guess he got to play a lot of golf.

George and I purchased a very cute, brand new house in Greens Farms, an area in Westport and we had a trucking company move all of my big new furniture from my apartment to our new house. A few of those pieces of custom furniture moved with me over the years and I can still remember exactly how I had it all set up in my apartment in New York.

Nevertheless, we were happily married in Westport and had a big reception for all of the members at the Longshore Club and in the evening we left for Pinehurst.

While George played and practiced at Pinehurst, I played at Mid-Pines Club and broke 100 for the first time.

George's good friend Frank Stranahan, a world class amateur title holder, was my first famous golfer to meet. Wow, was he handsome and so very nice. I was in heaven with my new husband and his golfing life and friends.

Next, I met Julius Boros and his wife Buttons. She was a very good golfer too. Ed Furgol and his wife, and by the time we got to California I had gotten to know so many Professionals. Sam Snead, Ben Hogan, Byron Nelson, Cary Middlecoff, Lloyd Mangrum, Jackie Burke, Vic Ghezzie, Manual De la Torre and so many more.

In those days, the wives were allowed to follow along with the playing Pros and it was certainly an education to see them playing so beautifully.

1951

One day when I was watching George practicing for the Los Angeles Open at the Riviera Club in Pacific Palisades, George insisted that I hit balls and practice right along side of him. I didn't want to because Ben Hogan, Sam Snead and Julie Boros were all practicing at that time. But I did hit a few balls and quit after a dozen or so. I didn't feel that I was in the right place for that and I was pretty much in awe of all professional golf at that time. We rented a nice apartment in Santa Monica, which is due west of Los Angeles, on Wilshire Boulevard. I had always enjoyed cooking and it was easier for us to have most of our meals in our apartment. No one can foresee the future but in a year or so, my family decided to move to California and they eventually bought their home in Santa Monica. They lived there the rest of their lives and I would take a trip out from the east annually for years and years.

There were several big golf tournaments in the Los Angeles area and one of them was played at Rancho Santa Fe on the outskirts of San Diego. George had some good friends who were formerly from Westport and now lived in a super mansion on Rancho Santa Fe. We stayed in their guest house and often went to the main house to have dinner with them. They were Sandy and Carl Schlate, and we called him Mr. Shell Oil. They had owned a magnificent estate in Westport called "Bluewater Hill" overlooking the Long Island Sound. They sold the estate when they moved west and it was subdivided into three or four smaller estates. The main house was bought by Nancy Black who loved to play golf and be at the Longshore Club. This house was terrific and had a bowling alley downstairs. The carriage house was bought by Jean and Bob Kintner. He was president of NBC and this was their country home. Jean was an avid golfer and one of my all time favorite ladies. I played quite a bit of golf with her over the years. She was also a member of Wee Burn Country Club in Darien, CT. Black Jack Bouvier, Jackie Bouvier Kennedy's uncle, was a member of Wee Burn.

Back to 1950 and the other places we played golf. Probably the club I loved the most was the Bel-Aire Golf Club in Beverly Hills. George had made friends with Dottie and William Wellman from his previous trips there. William Wellman was a famous movie director and his dear wife Dottie was the mother of their six children. Amazing, because she looked like a movie star herself and she was so very, very nice. I played golf with her at Bel-Aire and we had lunch there too. This club was so popular with all of the movie stars and still is. Sean Connery (James Bond) was a member and may still be. He is a fine golfer. Dean Martin was said to play golf there every day and he also was a fine golfer. It is such a beautiful club and very private. In fact there is a security gate for the Bel-Aire residences before you even get to the club. I think possibly that club set the pattern for later private clubs. It was all a great experience to be out there and be part of the elite golfing community.

1951

The winter tour moved on up to the San Francisco area for the Bing Crosby Invitational. This was indeed a very special event and loaded with all kinds of professionals. It was one of the most famous golf tournaments in the world and in fact it still is these many years later. Bing invited many celebrities including Phil Harris, Jack Lemmon, Bob Steele, and James Garner, just to name a few from that era. Today the Pro-Am consists of names like Alice Cooper, Bobby T, Kenny G, all musicians and many, many CEOs from the big corporations.

So after we arrived and found a place to stay, we went over to the practice area so George could hit balls, and guess who was hitting balls? My good friend Bob Crosby. He met George and we exchanged pleasantries and I didn't get to see him there again. But I did see him again a few years later.

While we were there, George looked up a good old friend, Hank Ketcham and his lovely wife Alice. Hank wanted to show us an idea he had for a comic strip called Dennis the Menace! Hank had been working for Walt Disney whose forte at that time was Mickey Mouse. Later when Dennis the Menace took off as a big hit, they moved back east again and we saw quite a lot of them and played golf with Hank, an avid golfer. We had good mutual friends from New York who also had a great country house in Connecticut, and we often played at other clubs in the area. Sadly, Alice died in the fifties and we all missed her. A decade later when George and I split, I dated Hank quite a lot and we had a good time. However, he moved to Switzerland for quite a long time and later moved back to Pebble Beach where he built a beautiful home on the Pebble Beach Golf Course. I am sure he was very happy there, but he too passed away in 2005.

The next stop on the tour was Tucson, Arizona and then on to Phoenix, Arizona. We were pretty much into a routine by now. I would drive George to the golf course where he would practice and then later go back and watch all of the goings on. The previous year when George was on the tour, he had played golf at the great Arizona Desert Biltmore Hotel in the heart of Phoenix. He had played in a Pro-Am and his partner was Clark Gable. He was impressed with Clark and enjoyed playing golf with him and also the fact that everyone else ate lunch and Clark ate only an apple! That took discipline. The following year when I was with George, again the tour stopped at Phoenix. I fell in love with that great hotel and it was my first knowledge of Architect Frank Lloyd Wright. Such a wonderful place. Quite a few years later, I had the opportunity to go to a party at a house he had designed in New Canaan, Connecticut. He certainly was one of a kind.

Next stop was San Antonio and I recall that George did well in that tournament. The tournament was played at Breckenridge Golf Club and the pros loved this course because the course was very dry and the ball would roll so fast that it made the course play shorter than usual. Back in the fifties golf courses did not usually have sprinkler systems. Now it is a rarity to see a course that does not have a sprinkler system.

Before long, it was getting to be the end of winter and time to be heading back home to Westport. We arrived home the first of March. At that point I was debating about going back to New York and my singing career but the golf bug had really bit me hard and I spent the bulk of my time practicing or playing golf. There are so many golf events in that area that I was always going to another club to play in a member-guest tournament or a guest day of some sort.

The summer passed quickly and before I knew it we were planning to go on the Winter Tour again at the end of October. In early October, I went with George to upstate Connecticut where he played in the Connecticut Open. There was a full field and the tournament was three days. I told George that I would have a surprise for him after the tournament was finished. I like to think he had a clue and was inspired because he WON! He was Connecticut State Champion in 1951. So my good news was that I was pregnant! How happy we both were! A couple of weeks later we left for the Winter Tour again starting in Pinehurst, North Carolina.

We stopped in San Antonio, Texas on our way west and George played golf with LPGA founder Betty Jamieson. One of the all time greats! Well, I tried to follow them as they played, but I was hit with such morning sickness that I would simply lie down in a rain shelter and wait until they came that way. I was practically living on salt free crackers.

We arrived in L.A. and my parents had made the move to California. My Mom and Dad came to watch George play in the L.A. Open. It was a great treat for them to see the beautiful Riviera Country

Club, a grand tradition. Remember that both of my parents played golf. I remember we were standing on the right side of the 18th fairway as George was playing the hole and he ran over to introduce us to Johnny Weismuller and his beautiful wife who were standing, watching, close to us. Johnny was an Olympic swimming medalist who became the first movie Tarzen!

1952

One night in February, we were in the theater watching a movie when I felt the baby move. I took George's hand and placed it on my belly and he felt it move. He got all excited and said in a loud voice "That is the most wonderful thing I've ever felt!" Everyone in the theater turned around and stared at us and wondered what it was that man had felt! Such a wonderful time of life. We were very happy!

Back in the world of television, the big new hit show was the "I LOVE LUCY" show, starring Lucille Ball and Desi Arnez. It was a smashing hit, very funny, and Lucille was pregnant with Desi Arnez, Jr. We had our babies about the same time and I watched that show every week and roared at the predicaments Lucy got herself into.

Soon again it was time to head home and I was five months pregnant. When we came up the New Jersey Turnpike there was such a massive snow storm in progress that it was very dangerous to drive and we had to stay overnight only three hours or so from home.

George Gordon Buck was born on June 30th at 4 PM. He was a week early and that was a sign of his personality to come, always rushing to get things done. One of my big life dreams was completed and the threads of the tapestry of life were still forming. I was a mother!

In October George was making plans to go on the winter tour again, but this time I was not going. I was pregnant with my second child and was also very busy enjoying taking care of George, Jr. George left for the tour with a golfing pro friend of his from Connecticut. In retrospect I realize that his friend was not a good influence. A couple of incidents later stuck in my mind as the beginning of playing overnight tournaments and chasing the ladies. George did not stay away as long as usual on the winter tour and came home in January. Everything was just fine with us and we were very happy with our little family.

1954

I spent the next couple of years with our two new babies. Gary Clayton Buck was born on August 14th, 1953. He was about ten days late and in the hospital, people wondered how come an older baby was in with the infants. He weighed eight and a half pounds. I had worked very hard on my nutrition and had only gained thirteen pounds all told. What a wonderful baby he was, and again the threads of my life tapestry were mounting up.

In the evening, I used to sing to the boys as they were going to sleep. One night after I had sung them to sleep, I started to cry as I realized my New York life was all behind me and I wouldn't be singing again. Well, that wasn't exactly the case, but at that time I felt it was.

George often played in Pro-Am tournaments in the Metropolitan area and often had some interesting partners. He played with Perry Como as a partner and he enjoyed that a lot. He said that his golf game was just the way he sang. Very relaxed and easy. In another tournament his partner was Sid Caesar and he raved about him. He was indeed one of the greatest all time funnymen and had millions of fans.

In the fall of this year, George took a winter job as Co-Pro at Harder Hall in Sebring, Florida. I guess that this hotel was built during the big building boom in the twenties and it was a wonderful Southern design a la the Breakers and many other resorts of that era. We bought a new trailer and towed it down to Florida and lived in it for the first winter. It was a great adventure and the boys loved the area even though they were still pretty small.

Sebring is a most charming little town and this year was the beginning of another building boom in that area. We enjoyed the fine resort and played golf on the town golf course that was right across the street from the main entrance to Harder Hall. They built their own Golf Shop adjacent to the Hotel immediately and in another year or two, the Harder Hall Golf Course was completed and open for play. A superior golf course, as good as any, and in fact though years later the Hotel closed, the golf course is still thriving and is host to some fine tournaments every year.

1955 - 1960

As the boys got older, we decided to buy a house for our winter home. It was a great house and we enjoyed it very much. We lived there for another six years or so. Soon the boys started school in Florida, and in April I would drive back to Connecticut and put them in school there for the rest of the year. Then in September it was the reverse order. George, Sr. traveled on his own in those days and actually spent fewer months in Florida than the boys and I did.

It was during this era that I worked on my golf swing and game. I also played a lot at the City of Sebring Course. I would get a sitter on

Wednesdays for after school. I would play ladies' day Wednesday mornings and then play with guests at Harder Hall in the afternoon. I did that 36-hole routine for a number of years. I also played in many tournaments in those days and started winning most of the time. One match play for the club championship, in the final round, I won every hole on the front nine and the tenth to win. I shot even par. Now as you may know the Sebring Grand Prix automobile race is held there every year and is quite a spectacle. One year the boys and I went out for the day to watch. We also took a helicopter ride. That was great.

One year the golf club at Sebring held a couples championship and it was very well done. My partner and I won and the prize was a beautiful big silver tray that was engraved with the Sebring Grand Prix Emblem. Soon, a good golfing friend and I started going up to Tampa and St. Petersburg to play in LPGA events. That was really great experience and I met Kathy Whitworth as she was starting out, and Judy Rankin, also getting her experiences on the tour. Also Mickey Wright, whom I had met before in Connecticut, Betsy Rawls, Carol Mann, Sandra Haney, Gloria Armstrong, all of the players from that era. The LPGA was becoming hot stuff and the crowds were coming out to watch. One of the founders of the LPGA was Patty Berg. She was a long time friend of mine and passed on in the year 2006. How sad to see her go. She gave the most informative and entertaining golf clinics of any other professional. I first became aware of Patti in Vancouver in the early forties. There was front page coverage of her visit to Vancouver and, although I had only played golf a few times, I wished I had been able to meet her. She was so great right from her first days. Of course I did meet her many years later and we had a long time friendship. What a golfing Lady she was! I have many cards and letters from her that I consider to be valuable souvenirs.

Another interesting story concerned Kathy Whitworth. She was an avid tennis player and her friends kept after her to play golf with them. She obliged and got bit by the golf bug first time out. She said that she never knew it could be such a hard game. Now in her later years, she is a record holder of some immensity.

Arnold Palmer was enormously popular at the time we played in the Tampa Open. In fact he was responsible for the television networks starting to cover the final day or two of golf tournaments. So here I was playing at Tampa and on the eighteenth hole, my second shot caught a bunker protecting the green right in front. One of my playing group said to me as we walked up to the green, "You better hit a good shot, you're on television." We were the last group of amateurs to come in just ahead of the Pros. Well I really concentrated and hit a good shot out of the bunker onto the green. I had to laugh, me on television again, how ironic. At this time the LPGA ran two national tournaments. One in Tampa, Florida and one in nearby town, St. Petersburg. I played in both of them in the amateur class. Nowadays the fields are full and there are very few amateurs playing in these tournaments. Some of the girls I was paired with went on to become Professionals and it was during this time that I gave some serious consideration to becoming a professional, but I just couldn't bring myself to make the move with two darling little boys that took much of my interest. One of the amateurs that I had the pleasure of playing with in these tournaments was Althea Gibson, the tennis great. She had retired from tennis and taken up golf. Boy, did I enjoy playing with her! She could hit a long ball and had a pretty good swing, but her problem was staying out of trouble. Still in all, it was so great to watch her. She lived in New Jersey until she passed on around 2004.

I continued to play a great deal of tournament golf. The Southern New England Championship which I won eight times, The Southern Connecticut Championship, and The Fairfield County Championship. I played and won so many tournaments it was becoming like a job. In 1960 the town of Westport bought the Longshore Country Club and it became a resident club. I was asked to be the first Ladies President and accepted. The years rolled on golfwise and familywise too. I frequently played golf at a city golf course in Stamford, CT. One day when I was playing a practice round for an upcoming tournament, we were playing a little slowly and decided to wait and let the foursome of men who were behind us play through. Well, guess who it was! Jackie Robinson, the baseball great. We were very impressed and he stopped to talk to us for awhile and about our upcoming tournament. That was a treat!

Back up in New England later that year, I was introduced to Mickey Wright over at Patterson Club in Fairfield. She had come to give a clinic to the lady members and I was invited. What a treat to meet Mickey. I can't emphasize how utterly charming and delightful she was. Possibly the best player of that era.

That same year, another member of the Patterson Club, Dr. Milton Lieberthal, who was very knowledgeable about music and Broadway Shows, apparently came forth with his ideas to recruit talent and present a show, "Longshore Follies". The club backed him all the way and rehearsals soon started. He hired a band from New York and a director from New York and we were off and running. I just loved how he did things and his ideas. He also was happy to have me aboard in a number of roles. The show was terrific and was loved by all. We had two beautiful and clever young girls, daughters of members at Longshore who performed in our Longshore Follies. They were Pam Martin, daughter of Margaret Martin, an avid golfer. Pam went to Hollywood and starred in the Nancy Drew series of movies and she was very successful. The other young lady was Tina Louise. A real stunner. She said to me, if only I could sing like you do. She was most famous for her part on the hit TV Show, Gilligan's Island, which ran for years.

Next year, Dr. Lieberthal produced Longshore Follies II. It again was a huge hit and we did it for two nights. Also quite a few people came to the dress rehearsal. This experience of performing and assisting the director was good for me because after doing the show for two years the good Doctor retired. So, I took over and directed and produced Longshore Follies III. It was called "Way Off Broadway" mimicking the Off Broadway shows that were so popular at that time. Again like my predecessor, I did the Follies for two years but it was such a demanding job that I could not do it again.

Back at Harder Hall for the winter, I ended up doing some floor shows for the Hotel. On Saturday nights they would hire a name act to come up from Miami and do the floor show. Usually a Headline Comic like Larry Best, George Kirby, Henny Youngman and Jackie Mason. He was a sketch. So funny and he enjoyed our local Joke Gang. One night, the Jacobson Brothers, who ran Harder Hall, asked me to step in because they had not been sent an act. They had a six piece band that played nights in the cocktail lounge after dinner and so they also played for me. Everyone loved it and they thought that they had a fine act on call, but they didn't even offer to pay me anything, so I wasn't too often available.

1960 -1963

These were busy years. They held the first Harder Hall Women's Invitational in January,1960. Good golfers from all over came and it was a very successful tournament. I think Marge Burns of North Carolina won. Possibly she won it more than once. She was a fine player. I also recall Barbara McIntyre playing in the event and Carol Mann. They were top amateurs in those days. This was a national tournament and a pretty big time tournament. One year I was medalist on the opening round but I never won the Harder Hall Invitational.

This tournament is still a favorite with the best golfers in the country and is held every year in January. My good friend Maureen O'Brien from Myrtle Beach, SC goes every year to play in the Harder Hall Invitational. Maureen and I had teamed up to play in many partners tournaments in the Carolinas in the eighties and nineties. She is still a superb golfer.

One year the new TV Show "Wonderful World of Golf" came to Harder Hall for a week or so. Bob Crosby was the host and I don't think there has ever been another golf host as super as he was. Very personable and intelligent, and he explained everything so well to the viewing audience. I never saw him again after that. He was a most talented gentleman. He was one of my most favorite people and he has gone on to that great concert hall in the sky.

In the early sixties, Arnold Palmer and his master-mind Mark McCormack came to Harder Hall for a few days. What a time that was!

They were both so personable and everybody got to know them quite well. Harder Hall was very much like a huge private club and we had the same guests winter after winter. So when we gathered in the lounge after golf, everybody knew everybody. A group of joke tellers grew amongst us and Dr. Ed Malmed from Philadelphia was the head man. He could tell jokes that literally had us falling off of our seats. One of his jokes actually fit our group so well about the new guy in prison who was joining in a group of story tellers and someone would say "SEVEN" and everyone would break out laughing. Then another guy would say "TWELVE" and again everyone would break into laughter. The new guy turns to his neighbor and says "I don't get it, what's with this SEVEN and TWELVE stuff?" His neighbor says "It's just that they have heard these jokes so many times that now they just tell them by the numbers." Well the Harder Hall gang never quite got to that but we would say, hey Doc, tell the one about the couple at the hotel on their 25th Wedding Anniversary.

I don't think that Arnold Palmer and Mark McCormack got into the joke telling but they did enjoy our members and the lounge and good food.

I was always a great admirer of Arnold Palmer, his game, his personality and his golf swing. When I was giving a lot of classes to beginner women golfers, I had a poster sized set of pictures of Arnold Palmer's hands showing the perfect way to grip the club. It was an excellent teaching tool. I had that poster for many years before it got lost somewhere while making a move. Arnold Palmer is probably the world's all time great professional athlete. He has played and won so many tournaments for the past sixty or so years. His personality and friendliness is very much admired by all and "Arnie's Army" must be the biggest Army in the world. He has nineteen Holes-In-One to his credit.

Another year at Harder Hall they held the Haig and Haig Scotch Foursome, which was a Professional Tournament with each team consisting of a Lady Pro and a Man Pro. This was a big tournament and was held for two or three years before the sponsor folded. One outstanding team I recall was Mickey Wright and Sam Snead. I don't believe that they got along too well and only teamed up one year. I guess that Mickey Wright was one of my all time favorite Pro golfers and I had the opportunity to attend a very small clinic she put on at a club in Westport. She is still a great golfing lady. Probably my favorite was Babe Didrickson Zaharias and there has never really been anyone person so endowed with athletic abilities. Back to Sam Snead. Sam was a hoot! He came into the lounge at night and played his trumpet with the band and generally was a lot of fun. He was double jointed and displayed his abilities by making a high kick to the top of the entrance door. Lots of fun in those days. I ran across Sam Snead a few times along the way and in the early eighties when Werner and I were members of the Long Cove Club on Hilton Head, Sam came one day and gave a clinic for the members. It wasn't too crowded and I was able to have a chat. He of course remembered me and George Buck from the Harder Hall days. Many of these people now are legends in their own time and I have felt most privileged to have met them.

Well, life moved on at a rapid pace and living in Westport certainly was interesting. There were a lot of celebrities who lived there. Zsa Zsa Gabor and her mother Jolie, who used to love to come over to the pool and beach area at Longshore in the summertime. Paul Newman and Joanne Woodward, who still live there, and it was not unusual to see either of them shopping or whatever. Martha Raye rented a house there one year, but I never ran across her. Bette Davis was there for a few years and one time she came around to a lot of tables at a dinner dance with an escort and said hello to everyone. She was so gorgeous and tiny and pleasant. What a pleasure to meet her. Famous actor David Wayne played golf at Longshore and loved to come into the club after golf and tell jokes. He later moved back to California and one winter when I was visiting my parents in Santa Monica, I bumped into David as he was coming out of a Travel Agency. His most famous role was with Marilyn Monroe in "How to Marry a Millionaire".

One day I had the pleasure of going to visit Sandy Dennis, the Oscar winning actress who lived in Weston, CT. There on the mantel shelf, nicely featured, was her Oscar. That was a real treat.

There were all kinds of tournaments to play at this time in my life and one of the most fun events was the mixed couples. Usually played on Sundays when the men were more available. You signed up and never knew who your partner would be for that day. One Sunday, I was paired with Eddie Anastasia, who was a fireman. His wife did not play and of course George did not play in these events. Well, it was a cold fall day and most of the men carried a bottle of scotch or something in their bags. They would take a little nip to beat the cold and by the time we got to the back nine they had convinced me to take a little nip too. Now I have always been a social drinker and that was the first and last time I ever took a nip while playing golf. I was okay through the first few holes, but by the time we got to the sixteenth hole I had developed the hiccups. On the seventeenth hole I fell down from the elevated tee and cut my shin and it was bleeding a lot. Eddie played the last two holes alone and I simply rode my way in. At the clubhouse, he got some ice and put it on my shin to stop the bleeding. Everyone thought it was hysterical except me. I can't explain how I had such a reaction to a little drink but it was sure a good lesson.

One day at Longshore, I was at the eighteenth green late in the day practicing my chipping to the flag. We were allowed to do that if no one was playing the eighteenth hole. A tall gentleman came out from the clubhouse and walked over to me and said, "Do you think you could teach me to chip like that?" Well, I was a little taken aback because it was Gregory Peck! They were making a film and using Longshore for some of their scenes. So I thanked him and suggested that he could take some lessons from George. So he thanked me and went back into the clubhouse. As it happened, at that same time, George was giving a refresher lesson to Pat O'Sullivan a fine amateur from New Haven, who had previously played as a touring LPGA member and then retired from that because she couldn't tolerate all of the traveling. She became reinstated as an amateur and won the State of Connecticut Championship a number of times. I played with her often and she was great. Anyhow, when she heard about Gregory Peck, she nearly fainted and we had to go up to the club and meet him.

BERYL BUCK

1964

The boys were getting older and involved in little league baseball, basketball and lots of other activities. This year I decided to make an adventurous trip to California. I had a brand new Cadillac and planned to drive across the country stopping at whatever tourist places that the boys wanted to see. I picked Grand Canyon, Disney Land and Yellowstone National Park. They picked Merrimac Caverns, Painted Desert, Meteor Crater, Petrified Forest, and we all picked Las Vegas. I did not play in the Club Championship that year. We were gone over a month. It was a wonderful trip full of great experiences and I am so glad that I pulled it off. On our return trip, we stayed at the Lodge in Yellowstone National Park. Early in the next morning we signed up for a horse trip into the park. After all the people were signed up, the leader rode down the line and stopped and said to me, "You look like you know how to ride a horse, go back and pull up the rear." Both of my boys said "MOM!" I had ridden quite a bit in my teens as well as that summer at Banff. They had also ridden a few times so they knew how to ride. What a good memory. Soon we started driving back east and it was good to get home.

Before I knew it, it was time to go to Florida. Little did I know what was in the offing. No need to go into details now, suffice it to say that a very disturbing incident with George and a girl friend was the straw that finally broke this Camel's back.

1966

By the spring of this year, we were divorced and it took a lot of concentration to make my boys accept the fact that it was not their fault. I had an open door policy with them and their Dad and it seemed to work out pretty good. It wasn't easy but life does go on. One positive development of this change in our lives was that we no longer went to Florida for the winter and so we took up Ice-Skating and Skiing. I had done both before, but the boys were novices. In fact, when I was working at NBC Studios at Rockefeller Center, I bought a pair of ice skates and used to go skating at the Rockefeller Rink. We had some great one day ski trips up in New England, and George in particular became a fine skier by the time he was eleven or twelve years old. Gary never really liked the cold weather and he preferred ice-skating. I don't recall the exact year, but we took an ambitious trip to Montreal for the World's Fair. That was such a great trip and so educational. One day we were watching a theatre in the round all about Canada and her best big cities. When the lights came on I was shedding a few tears and the boys both said, "What's wrong Mom?" So I explained how the show had made me sad that I was no longer a Canadian citizen and was reminiscing all about my life in Canada. But I was very happy with my American life and my two wonderful boys. In fact when I was pregnant with George was when I became an American Citizen. I was teased that the Government got two for one.

Within a year or so, I decided to supplement my income and took on some singing jobs in the area with small groups. It was great and I did enjoy doing club work again, but it wasn't the same as being single and living in New York. I was offered two or three different jobs hosting, etc. but it didn't quite seem right. One day I went up to the radio station WICC which was headquartered in Bridgeport and had a branch office in Fairfield. I thought there might be something in that field that I had not explored. Well, there really wasn't, but I did get to meet John Metts who was Vice-president of the radio station and we became quite friendly along with his beautiful wife and attended some social activities together.

The Big Band of Stan Kenton was playing an engagement at the ballroom of a big hotel in Bridgeport and I made plans to meet John and his wife at that location with a nice gentleman that I was dating at that time. We got there first and were sitting at our table when they came in. I said to my date, "Here they come now!" He said, "You never told me they were black!" Well I never thought about it and it was just as well. Stan Kenton came over to our table later and he was very interesting. An all time Jazz Great! His band was about seventeen pieces and played some wonderful selections. Well we all got along famously and were invited to a black fraternity party a few weeks later and we were the only white people there. We had a great time. Through John, I met Jerry Simon who headed up his own record company, RSVP, headquartered in New York. We became good friends for many years and his recording sessions were always fun to attend. Meadowlark Lemmon of the Harlem Globetrotters became one of Jerry's talents and he sang just like Nat King Cole. His record of "Personality" was a big hit. When I started teaching golf, Meadowlark came for some lessons and his wife came too. We were invited to go see a Harlem Globetrotters game at a stadium in Westchester and sat on the front line. Such an exciting night that was and the Globetrotters were spectacular.

Even though George and I were divorced, we remained friendly and he would come over to see the boys frequently. One year he invited me to be his partner in a Pro-lady tournament held at New City Golf Club which was over the Tappan Zee Bridge in New York. It was a tri-state event. New York, New Jersey and Connecticut. Well we teamed up very well and were runners-up in the final match. The winning couple was Harry Dee and his partner. Harry was formerly the Head Pro at this club and knowing such tricky greens was certainly to his advantage. George won money and I won a beautiful gold charm with a diamond in the middle. What a prize!

Another couple that I enjoyed meeting was Tommy Bolt and his partner LaJunta White. Years later when my husband Werner and I moved to the Long Cove Club in Hilton Head, it was my pleasure to renew my friendship with LaJunta. She was now married to Lou Stovall and they were very active golfers in those days.

Around 1968 George took a winter job at Doral in Miami, FL. He insisted we come down for a visit and it was a great visit to a great place. I even got to play "The Blue Monster" course. This wonderful resort was built by Al Kaskel and was named for him and his wife Doris, hence DORAL. After his death in the eighties his son took over. Al owned a charming farm in Stamford, CT and one day we went there for a visit. Another resort where George took a winter job was the "El Conquistador" in Fajardo, Puerto Rico. It would take several pages to describe this most outstanding and fantastic place, and I consider myself very lucky to have been invited to visit there. The design of El Conquistador was one of a kind. A Mediterranean style Hotel with many different outdoor levels and a pool at each level. They had a funicular cable car that ran downhill to a spacious beach and pool. Some friends who were visiting from Connecticut convinced me to sing with a good Latin band playing at an outdoor pool. So I sang "The Girl From Ipanima" and "Quiet Nights" – both Latin songs. They loved it. At night the ballroom was spectacular with a big Bandstand at each end and two bands that alternated. Every chair, and there must have been a thousand of them, was upholstered in green patent leather and NO TWO WERE ALIKE! They also had a Green Volkswagen that was upholstered in the same leather. Spectacular.

    Back to Doral in Miami. One night when George was up in front of the band and singing his favorite song, "King of the Road", he kept forgetting the words and the band kept feeding him the words as he sang, a voice from the back of the lounge hollers out, 'STOP'. It was Jackie Gleason, who played Doral nearly every day. He came up to the bandstand and said, "George, you stick to golf and stop butting into my business. Let me show you how to sing a song." He then proceeded to sing two or three songs while George sat down and listened. Jackie Gleason lived in Miami and was a regular golfer at Doral. He had a golf cart specially rigged up that had a bar on the back. He had a great personality and was everybody's pal. To this day Doral is a favorite stop on the PGA Tour.

Part Three
My LPGA days

Over the years many friends had said they wish I would teach golf and in thinking about that a light went on! A new Arnold Palmer facility was opening up on the Boston Post road in Westport and so I went up and introduced myself and took a brochure of information with me including some copies of my newspaper column, 'THE HAPPY GOLFER'. They were happy to have me aboard and thus began my career as a golf teacher. I was amazed at how busy I became and in no time I had a waiting list. I loved this new career. Incidentally, I wrote that "Happy Golfer" golf column faithfully every week for more than ten years. It was so interesting to see students get results and I started hearing stories about how well they did this and that.

I started a WORKING GIRLS CLASS on Monday evenings after work and they loved it. Also I had a few handicapped golfers come to me for help and that was a challenge. Quite a few juniors came for lessons and I had students of every age, sex and experience. By now I was a member of the LPGA and their offices were in New York City, so one day I went in to see their operation. They told me that I was the only member who had come into their New York Office. Their office was previously located in Atlanta, Georgia on Peachtree Street. It wasn't too long before they moved again, this time to Sugarland, Texas and their playing course was Sweetwater Country Club. About fifteen years ago, they moved again to the area west of Daytona Beach, Florida, and this is now their permanent home.

I soon became a Class A Pro and was appointed as an Area Representative. This meant that I would administer written exams to new applicants. The practical exams were usually done at seasonal seminars. I was often the guinea pig student because I had started out a left-handed golfer and that was a good test to see if the new applicant had a handle on teaching lefties. Also, it was so many years ago for me that I wasn't good as a Leftie. Ah the memories. One of our outstanding new members in the Northeast section of the LPGA was Jane Frost from Massachusetts. She was all full of enthusiasm and became an outstanding member. Now, decades later, she has her own golf school in Massachusetts. And her own plane, and she will fly to other parts of the USA to give clinics and instruction. She was very upset with me when I retired from the LPGA in 1986, but she also understood my situation. Another outstanding Lady Pro was Lorraine Klippell, who had also come from Canada. She was a great gal and I believe she now lives in Florida and Pennsylvania.

The boys were growing up and one of their friends was Joel Douglas, son of Kirk Douglas. The Douglas' lived in Westport and sometimes I would pick up Joel and Kirk would stand at the door and wave goodbye as we drove away. I think Kirk's wife's name was Ann and they were a nice family to have living in Westport. Joel was over at our house a lot and he was a nice young man.

Another nice resident in Westport was Martha Stewart and she lived on Turkey Hill Road, just one block away from us. She started out as a caterer in Westport. She is an enormously talented lady with millions of ideas. She still keeps that house on Turkey Hill Road, even with all of her other homes. She loved to grow a garden and have animals at her place. I can't say as I recall ever having met Martha. Too bad, my mother's name was Martha.

Teaching golf was a great livelihood for me and I had never dreamed how busy I would be. I also started teaching at Longshore Country Club on Saturdays and before too long I was also helping out with the Junior golf classes that George ran in the summer months. What a lot of fun that was working with those young kids. He ran about ten classes each week and they were full.

In the fall of 1966 or 1967 I was approached by the Physical Education Director of Staples High School to see if I would be interested in starting up a girls' golf team and being the coach. Yes, I accepted that opportunity and that was a top-notch experience. It was a brand new idea and several other state schools also started a girls' golf program. When we played elsewhere, I would drive four girls and someone's mother would drive four girls. I took the whole team on a field trip to see an LPGA tour event at Wykagil Golf Club in Westchester County. They loved it. Also one day we were at Longshore Country Club in Westport and as we were getting organized to play, Jim McKay came off the golf course and I introduced him to all of the team. He was one of the all time great Sports Announcers. Our team was very good and some of those girls went on to become outstanding golfers. One became a club champion in Westport. One moved to Massachusetts and became a good state golfer and one moved to Florida and joined the LPGA. I coached the team for about four years and then had to give it up due to lack of time. But we were pioneers in that activity.

1968-1969

During these years I was working pretty hard at my profession and enjoying it very much. Some of my students were remarkable. A lady who was a retired nurse and suffering from Parkinson's disease decided that some golf lessons might help her physically. At the Arnold Palmer practice range, students would purchase a bucket of balls and carry them out to where I held forth. This lady said to me. "If I drop anything or fall down on my way out, don't come and help me, I'll manage." It was about fifty yards out under a big tree. I just loved this woman. I would give her the fundamentals relative to her learning curve. She would try this or that, shaking uncontrollably all the time. Then address the ball, still shaking. As soon as she started her backswing she stopped shaking and could hit the ball very well. What an experience. Another lady who was equally determined to learn how to play did not have a left thumb. No one would ever know because you cover your thumb with you right hand, but of course she had to manage without very much strength in her left hand. She was a great person and became a nice golfer.

Another gentleman had a difficult problem. His practice swing was just fine, but put the ball down and he turned from Mr. Hyde to Dr. Jekyl. He would make a completely different swing, trying to kill the ball. We did get some better results, but I wonder if he was able to hang on to what we were doing. Quite a few couples would come for joint lessons and it seemed to work for them, but the ideal lesson is one on one.

What are the most common problems?

First of all, alignment. Golf is a target game and most new golfers will aim too far to the right.

Secondly, tempo. Watch the Touring Pros. You do not often see them swinging too fast…Hard maybe, but not too fast.

Third, not keeping a steady center to the swing. When Jack Nicklaus was building his game, he had his teacher hold his head steady, by holding his hair. If you think about your shoulders coming under your chin, it will help.

When you start a woman from scratch, she can usually hit the ball pretty straight, but she cannot get it airborne. Men are just the opposite. They can fly the ball all over the place, but they cannot hit it straight.

One Pro Golfer that I believe should be mentioned, because of her unusual approach to hitting the ball, is Annika Sorenstam. She doesn't worry about keeping her head steady, but simply follows the ball. It is a good theory and worth trying. Her coach had her try this theory when she was learning and it worked so well for her that she has retained it in her swing. "Keep your head down" is a phrase that should be outlawed. You work to keep the center of your swing steady and keeping your eye on the ball is the answer. Even if you follow the ball as Annika does, you do not ever want to pull up, but swing through! This idea of following the ball works very well for some golfers when putting. Maybe worth a try to see if it works for you.

One day I went to Bloomingdales in Stamford, Connecticut, to hear a lecture by the Editor-In-Chief of Golf Magazine. I went with Jean Hacker. She and her husband Charles were half owners of the Arnold

Palmer Practice Facility where I taught. After sitting there for about twenty minutes, the lady in charge of those events got up to the microphone and said, "Well it looks like we are not going to have a speaker today." I pulled out my LPGA card and went up and said, "Maybe I can help." She said, "Great, go ahead." So I gave a thirty-minute lecture on the object of the game, etc. and it went very well. A few days later, she sent me a story from the Stamford Paper of how I saved her life, and then she called and arranged for me to come again and be the featured speaker. Of course I did and it was very successful and I appreciated every bit of it. One more mention here. My friend Jean Hacker is a great lady and I enjoyed a fine friendship with her over the years. Charles Hacker was Vice-President of Radio City Music Hall in New York City. Absolutely the most magnificent theatre in the world.

I continued to write my "Happy Golfer" column and it was now in four or five newspapers, including one in West Palm Beach, Florida. I was also kept pretty busy doing appearances and lectures here and there. Often when I gave a golf lecture in front of an audience, I would conclude by hitting plastic balls into the audience and then afterwards, replacing them with a good golf ball.

One day I had a phone call from a guy who was a Big Band Leader and he asked if he could come over and talk about something. Well, it seems that he was looking for a girl singer. I wasn't really too interested but thought that I might give it a try. Then he said that I would need a new photograph and he would make the arrangements. He said that he wanted a topless picture and that was the popular thing to do at that time. Well, of course, he was nuts and way out of line. I said "No thanks and goodbye." I never heard from him again. What a joke!

1970

In the spring of this year I decided to go to the PGA business school and get their degree. Business School I had decided to allow women to attend their classes. I was the first woman to attend and this class was held at Atlantic City. Having been there twice with Hi, Lo, Jack and the

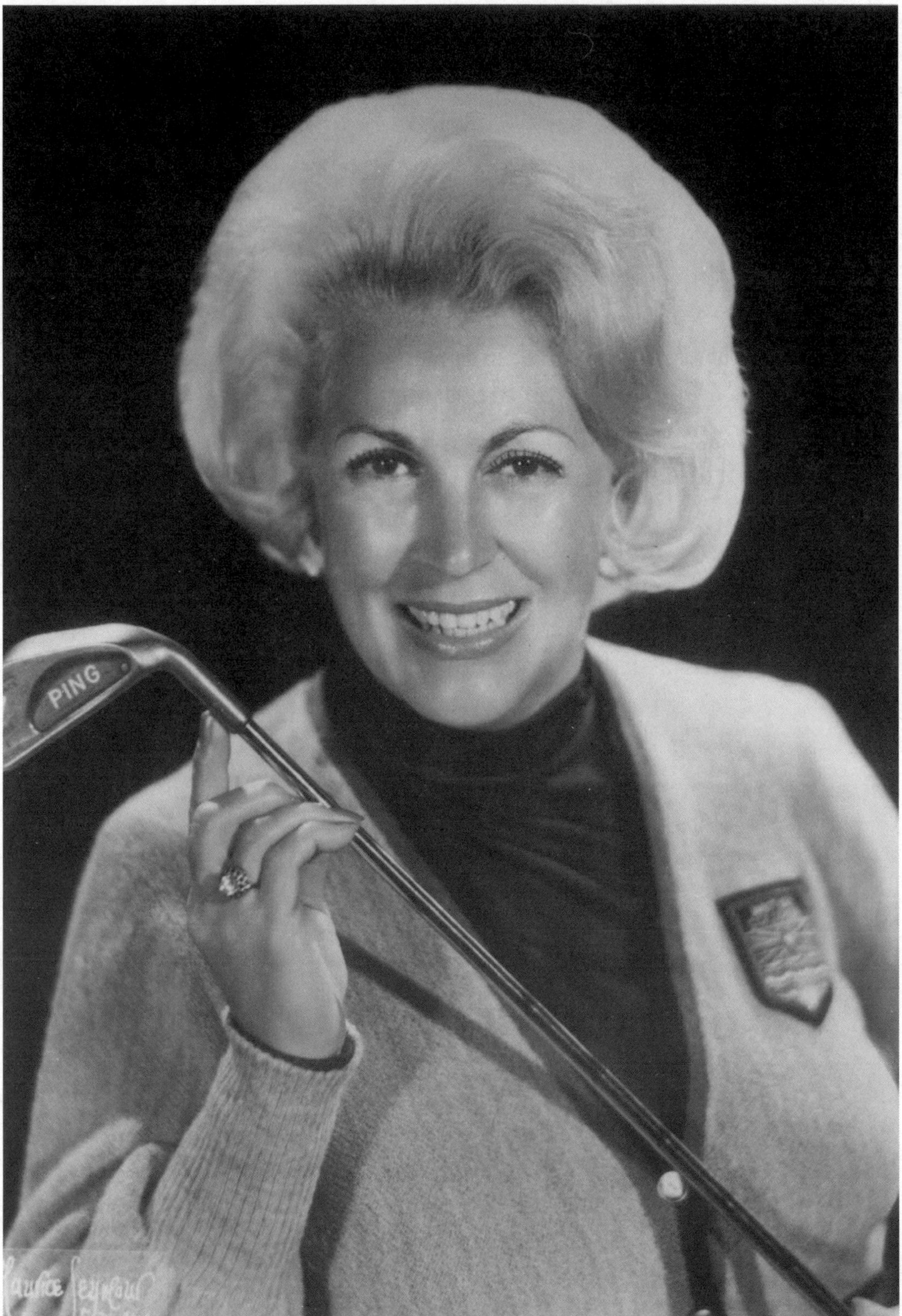
PING

Dame it was doubly interesting to me to go there. It was five days and five nights of classes and very interesting. On the final day, they had a photographer come to take the class picture. They asked me to move to the back of the room and out of the picture. I was stunned! After all I had worked just as hard as anyone else, paid the same money to take the class and taken the final exam and yet even though they had opened the door to women, I was not to be in the picture. Dr. Gary Wiren was running the classes and I was surprised to think that he would have allowed such discrimination. After the picture was taken and the class dismissed, about ten of the other students came up to me and said they were sorry for the turn of events. But nothing could be done.

During the spring of this year I was introduced to a very nice gentleman from New York City and we started dating regularly. By the end of summer we were engaged and planned a wedding for November. We went to Europe for a great honeymoon, first to London, then Paris, and finally Madrid. My first trip to Europe. We had a grand time and his brother, who lived in England, also went to Paris with us. He later moved to Paris. Then we returned home for Christmas and all of the Holiday Parties. One incident that made an impression on me happened at the Louvre Museum in Paris. We had gone there to see the Mona Lisa especially, and of course other great art. Standing in the main entrance and I guess waiting for his family was English actor-comedian, Terry Thomas. I was a big fan and loved the movie "The Magnificent Men and Their Flying Machines" which is now a classic. I was just a few feet from him and so I mouthed the words, "I Love You". He smiled and said "Thank You Very Much" in his typical English Accent. He made my day. Some years later I was sent a letter asking for help for Terry Thomas who was destitute and dying from some incurable disease. How Sad! Needless to say I sent a donation.

1971

This again was a busy year for me and I continued to teach golf and coach the Girls' Golf Team to another successful year of competition. My husband commuted to New York City daily and we spent evenings and weekends together. We were both fond of swimming and had a few parties at my swimming pool at my home. We also played golf on weekends and compared to my former life I wasn't getting to play very much golf. However it was my choice to continue teaching and I enjoyed it very much. How rewarding to get results for aspiring golfers. The year wore on and somehow or other our marriage also was wearing thin. We just seemed to drift apart and to this day I am not sure what exactly went wrong but it did. We chalked it up to experience and by the end of the year we had split up. We stayed pretty friendly for awhile but then lost touch. After that experience, I decided that three strikes were out and that I would not marry again. I was even toying with the idea of moving to California sooner or later. But it was not to be.

In the middle seventies, I started dating and playing golf with a very talented gentleman from New York who was a widower and lived in a great Tudor House in Westport. His name was Johnny Marks and he owned a music publishing house in the City. It was called Christmas Music. Why? Because he was the writer of the music for "Rudolph the Red Nosed Reindeer" and some other Christmas songs. He made a fortune with his music. We had a friendly relationship, not at all romantic and it was surprising to me when, at a party with my husband Werner sometime in 1978 where Johnny Marks was also a guest, that he made the following comment when introduced to Werner. He said, "She married the wrong man." One time in the middle seventies when my mother was visiting me at my home another funny incident happened with Johnny Marks. He came over to my house, walked into the living room and changed the channel on the television, and then walked over and sat down at the piano. My mother had been watching a program on the TV so he sure got off on the wrong foot with her. So, he was rattling off some good music on my Steinway and I said to my mother, "Doesn't he play well?" She replied, " I don't care if he played with his toes, I don't like him." Well she didn't have to worry because although I admired his talents, I was not enamored with him, so we soon stopped going out.

In the spring of 1974 I was contacted by someone from ABC in New York to come in and make an appearance on the Virginia Graham Show, a daytime show. So I went and Tom Seaver's wife was also a guest on the show. She became a theoretical student on live TV and I gave her a quick lesson. Tom Seaver was the Hot Star Pitcher for the New York Mets and in some ways made that team what it was. Well, that was fun. I believe that contact came from my "Happy Golfer" golf column.

"Claudia and David." (1946) Further adventures of Rose Franken's scatterbrained housewife. Dorothy McGuire, Robert Young, Mary Astor, Gail Patrick. (90 min.)
21 ELECTRIC COMPANY—Children
49 SESAME STREET
10:30 **2** **3** GAMBIT—Game
4 **20** JEOPARDY!—Game
5 MOTHERS-IN-LAW—Comedy
The Hubbards and Buells are all thumbs as they try to build a nursery for the baby. Eve: Eve Arden. Kaye: Kaye Ballard.
8 PASSWORD—Game
Susan Oliver and Bill Cullen.
21 MAN BUILDS, MAN DESTROYS
67 TRIM AND SLIM—Exercise
11:00 **2** **3** NOW YOU SEE IT—Game
4 **20** WIZARD OF ODDS—Game
5 I LOVE LUCY—Comedy (BW)
It looks like a peaceful trip back to New York—until Lucy gets involved with a jewel thief. Lucille Ball, Desi Arnaz, Vivian Vance.
7 GOMER PYLE, USMC—Comedy
Carter tries to meet the bikini-clad beauties Gomer appeared with in a magazine. Gomer: Jim Nabors. Carter: Frank Sutton.
8 SPLIT SECOND—Game
9 STRAIGHT TALK
Cuisine—from the basics to gourmet. Experts describe various types of cookery expertise. (60 min.)
21 SESAME STREET
67 CHEF NICOLA—Cooking
11:30 **2** **3** LOVE OF LIFE—Serial
4 **20** HOLLYWOOD SQUARES
Guests include Lynn Redgrave, Harvey Korman, Pearl Bailey, Martin Milner, Rob Reiner, Rose Marie, Paul Lynde and Charley Weaver.
5 MIDDAY LIVE
Kay Gilman interviews the wives of athletes; golf tips from Nancy Seaver and Beryl Buck. (Live; 90 min.)
7 **8** BRADY BUNCH
A compliment from Don Drysdale goes to Greg's head. Greg: Barry Williams. Mike: Robert Reed.
11 ABBOTT AND COSTELLO (BW)
The boys are loose at an auction.

AFTERNOON

12:00 **2** YOUNG AND THE RESTLESS—Serial
3 NEWS
4 **20** JACKPOT!—Game
7 PASSWORD—Game
Susan Oliver and Bill Cullen.
8 NEWS—Tom Kirby
9 LUCY SHOW—Comedy
To help Mooney escape an infatuated female, Lucy poses as his wife. Nanette: Edie Adams.
11 NEW ZOO REVUE—Children
What is happiness?
13 MASTERPIECE THEATRE
21 ELECTRIC COMPANY—Children
31 BRIAN SHAROFF
67 NASSAU/SUFFOLK WOMAN
12:25 **3** EYE ON WOMEN
12:30 **2** **3** SEARCH FOR TOMORROW—Serial
4 **20** CELEBRITY SWEEPSTAKES—Game
Joey Bishop, Gavin MacLeod, Kay Ballard, Ross Martin, Anita Gillette.
7 SPLIT SECOND—Game
8 WHAT'S MY LINE?
Gene Rayburn, Anita Gillette, film critic Leonard Harris and Arlene Francis.
9 BEVERLY HILLBILLIES (BW)
The Clampetts' dress shop opens at dawn to beat the competition. Jed: Buddy Ebsen. Granny: Irene Ryan.
11 MAGIC GARDEN
21 MISTER ROGERS' NEIGHBORHOOD
31 CASPER CITRON
12:55 **4** **20** NBC NEWS—Edwin Newman
1:00 **2** WHAT'S MY LINE?
3 MATCH GAME
Betty White, Bobby Van, Elaine Joyce, Brett Somers, Richard Dawson.
4 CONCENTRATION
5 MOVIE—Drama (BW)
"Alias Nick Beal." (1949) An attempt at allegorical fantasy, with an honest judge (Thomas Mitchell) rising in politics with the help of the Devil (Ray Milland). Martha: Wall. Donna: Audrey Totter. Ben: Henry O'Neill. Gaylord: George Macready. (2 hrs.)

TV GUIDE A-83

I continued on with my golf career and all was well in my life and the lives of my two boys who by now were pretty well out on their own. My "Happy Golfer" golf column attracted some attention and a publisher suggested that I put it into a book somehow or other, so I started working on that project. The years were rolling by and life was interesting. One day I was invited to a ladies golf luncheon at the Greenwich Country Club and the guest of honor was Golf Pro Kathy Whitworth. The lady at the microphone also recognized me from the floor. One of the ladies at the table I was sitting at said, "Oh, Mrs. Buck, I have always enjoyed all of your books for so many years." I was embarrassed to have to correct her and tell her that my name was not Pearl Buck, but Beryl Buck and also I was sure that Pearl Buck was no longer living.

My friend in New York, Jerry Simon, was having some success with his record company and also had met a darling and lovely lady named Celeste. She was a singer actress and soon they made a recording for her. They soon became engaged and were married in the City in 1982. Their friend Peter Paul from the city also became my friend, with his wife Shirley, and they all used to come up to Westport on weekends in the summer and stay over. We had a lot of fun. Peter Paul was very active in the world of entertainment and managed some top notch personalities. He suggested and prodded me to write a Golf Instruction book based on my weekly golf column "The Happy Golfer". So I did in fact start to put the book together and it took a lot of work and many hours of my time. However, I never did regret that endeavor and the book eventually was published and received very well.

After we had moved to South Carolina in 1981, we constantly tried to get Peter to come down for a visit and to play golf at the Long Cove Club where we first settled in South Carolina. After seven years there we moved to DeBordieu in Georgetown on the Atlantic Ocean. We still kept after Peter to come down and visit us and play golf. He was indeed planning to come in the spring of 1991 and he never made it. His son sent us a letter saying that Peter had dropped dead in that year. How sad!

1976

In the late winter of this year I was invited to a huge house party and inasmuch as I was single and went alone, I pitched in to help the bartender make drinks for the large number of guests. It was a great party with a trio playing for dancing and so on. A nice tall gentleman came up to the bar and his first words to me were, "Can you make me a martini?" Well, I did and then a little later he came and asked me to dance. I was quite impressed with him and a few days later he called and asked me to dinner. It wasn't easy being single and some of the dates I had were pretty sad. I don't recall going out with anyone a second time until now. His name was Werner Miller and we started a busy, busy relationship. He was impressed with my golf career and I was impressed with his career as a Builder-Developer. Of all the men I had dated, he was so far above the field that I soon fell for him. He was a widower and lonely. To make a long, long story shorter, we married in September, 1977. All good things come to he who waits!

We have traveled a great deal. To the Orient, Hawaii, Switzerland three or four times to ski and so on. We are happily ensconced in our home in Belfair and couldn't ask for anything more. When we first married, Werner was taken with the idea that I was a Professional Golfer and soon became my student. He had not played previously but was a natural. We often played at Banksville, NY and one day Werner had a Hole-In-One. How exciting. But the best Hole-In-One I have ever heard of was when we lived at DeBordieu in Georgetown, SC. It was a men's interclub golf day at DeBordieu and Werner had a Hole-In-One on the eighth hole. And guess what! It was Werner's Birthday, October first. Well he didn't have to buy any drinks because it was an open bar for the tournament.

At this time, Werner had become a five handicap golfer. We both stayed single digit golfers for a number of years.

WE MADE IT!
GREAT WALL
OF CHINA.

Skiing Is Believing

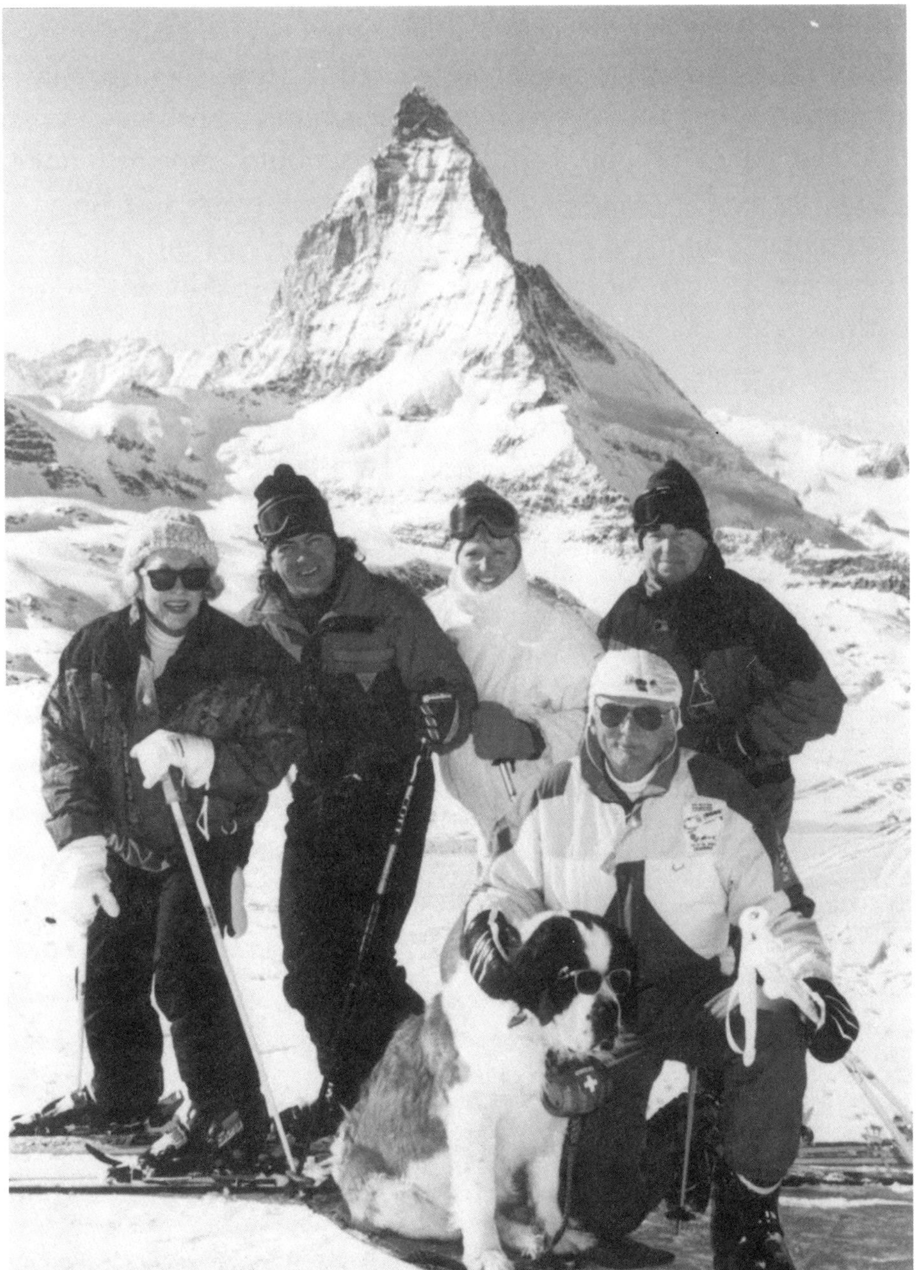

1978

In this year, the LPGA held one of their tour events at the Stanwich Country Club in North Greenwich, Conn. They sent out requests for help in running this event and I volunteered. I became a dispatcher of automobiles to drive the contestants to their hotels. That was a pretty enlightening experience. Some of the players would come into our office and demand a car instantly and if none were available, they would complain. Some of them were the other side of the coin and very nice. Best and most friendly of all was Nancy Lopez. She was so generous with her time. What a champion she is!

Another significant event happened around this time; my golf instruction book was published and very well received. It is now out of print and I understand that a few copies are for sale on E-BAY.

PLAY A ROUND
with Beryl Buck Miller

Beryl Buck Miller, L.P.G.A.

1980-1988

At some point in the early eighties, I was invited to come up to Connecticut and receive an award as Sportswoman of the year. They gave me an original etching of me with an interesting background, which I hang in my office. Very nice and thoughtful.

I was still enjoying teaching golf and we made some interesting trips to various places where the LPGA would be holding national seminars. From Cape Cod to Texas to Pennsylvania and more, these trips were great. Soon I achieved my Master Professional status, and then very soon after that I decided to retire from teaching. We were members of the Long Cove Club on Hilton Head Island, where Jim Feree was the director of golf. He is quite an excellent player and played on the Champions' Tour until very recently. When he first started at Long Cove, his assistant was Karen Shapiro, a fine golfer from Atlanta. She moved on to become the Head Pro and soon she and Jim became married. Now a re-instated amateur, Karen Shapiro has won many championships in the area. The head Golf Pro now at Long Cove is Bobby Patton. A very terrific guy and Nephew of Billy-Joe Patton an outstanding amateur from the fifties and sixties.

Now, even though I had applied to be reinstated as an amateur, I had not played a lot of golf for over twenty years and so I proceeded slowly upon reentering the world of state championship play. When I retired, I was Vice-President of the Northeast section of the LPGA and, although my professional career was drawing to a close, it had been a wonderful twenty or so years teaching and helping others. It is not an easy process to be re-instated as an amateur. You have to file a lot of paperwork and affidavits testifying on your behalf. Not everyone can be re-instated. If you have been serving others, you qualify. If you were simply polishing you own apple, you may not be accepted.

One of the first competitive events that I entered was on the Match Play Teams played from one club to another. My partner was Mildred Woods and I was impressed with her swing, her game and her personality from day one. We teamed up beautifully and I believe in all of those matches, we were unbeaten.

When we first moved to Hilton Head Island in 1981 I was surprised to see so many different kinds of events available. I joined the Hilton Head Choral Society who at that time was led by a lady named Martha. It was fall and time to start practicing THE MESSIAH. How wonderful this experience was and for me it was new to sing great classical music. In a few years, Martha retired and John Carter and his beautiful wife took over the Choral Society. We were developing into a year around program and it was a challenge for all of us. Along about the same time I joined a group called "The Island Singers". This group sang more contemporary music and a lot of music from Broadway Shows. I believe there were about twenty of us and our conductor was Judy Gallagher. We even did a theatre performance to a sell out audience. So the singing continued to roll on in my life.

I was playing in a one-day golf event at Litchfield Country Club in Myrtle Beach, SC with a really good player and a terrific lady, Maureen O'Brien. She later told me that she went over to her boyfriend who was following along and said "Isn't that Beryl Buck that I am playing with, from Connecticut?" She had originally come from Connecticut and remembered me from there. Well, we became very good friends and teamed up to play in many, many golf events and usually won. She is now married to her friend, Lamar Adams and still lives in Myrtle Beach.

I never played in the club championship at Long Cove Club, but Werner and I did play in the Couples' Championship once around the middle eighties and I recall that on the second day, I shot a 69. My third time to do so, but it had been a long time since I first did it.

One time Maureen and I teamed up with one other lady and our Pro from DeBordieu, John Abernethy, and we won that tournament handily too. By now we had built again and moved to DeBordieu, which is in Georgetown on the Atlantic Ocean. Quite a place! I was now playing a lot of state golf and won the South Carolina Super Senior championship three consecutive years. I also played in our DeBordieu Ladies Championship and won that handily a few times.

So my golf came back pretty much to where I had left off many years before. I signed up to play in the USGA Women's Senior Championship which was to be held in Georgia at the Cloisters Golf Club. I was up to a five or six handicap and able to qualify. Nowadays, you probably wouldn't qualify for this international tournament unless you were a scratch player. This is a great club, Sea Island Golf Club. The teaching pro there was Louise Suggs, one of golf's all time greats. I recall seeing her play in the Women's Open when it was played at Brooklawn Country Club in Fairfield, Connecticut in the mid 1970s. She certainly was a fine player. Now this is indeed one of the world's best golf tournaments. One of my fine friends from Myrtle Beach, Carolyn Cudone, still holds the record for the most wins of any USGA tournament. Now she was some golfer, too. A member of the Curtis Cup Team, and I had the pleasure of playing with her in some team events in South Carolina in the eighties.

So here I am playing in the Women's Senior Championship and this story will really get you going. It is three rounds. The second round I am paired with a very nice lady from California who according to local gossip is a man with a sex-change operation under her belt. No Pun! Boy, could she hit a ball. After all even though she was now a woman, she had the longer arms, thicker wrists and bigger hands of a man. She was nice and slender, but a different build than the rest of us. After the final round, there was a big fancy dinner at the Cloisters. Werner and I

INSTANT LESSON

Beryl Buck Miller
LPGA professional
Longshore C.C.
Westport, Conn.

PUT YOUR SWING TO MUSIC FOR IMPROVED TEMPO

Many golfers always are working to slow down their backswing. Actually, they should establish an overall pace or rhythm for the whole swing. I tell my students to swing to the timing of a familiar melody or song. Personally, I like the beat of the "Oom Pa Pa" band. Just make sure it's three-quarter or waltz time. Most golfers are swinging double time —much too fast. "Take Me Out to the Ball Game" and "Casey Would Waltz With the Strawberry Blonde" are good possibilities.

When you find a melody you like, swing the club back and forth continuously at least 10 times, with that tune in mind. Work on the overall tempo of your swing, rather than trying to slow down separate parts.

entered the dining room, which was set up with all tables for eight, and there is my golfing lady sitting alone. So we went over and sat with her. Another couple of ladies joined us but the table did not fill up. After the dinner, she was the first to leave and we were swamped with all of the golfers coming up to our table and asking us all about her and what she had to say and on and on. I felt badly for her and only had good things to say to the others. What was the upshot of all of this? On the application for this tournament in subsequent years, it always said, to be eligible a competitor had to be born as a woman to be accepted! End of story. That's the USGA, everything spelled out!

At this time we lived in DeBordieu in Georgetown, which is a great club. I was not only busy with a lot of golf, but started a singing group at the club. We sang at many club events and it was just wonderful. The members of this group were all very interested in our singing and one couple, Betty and Bob Kilgore, promised to join my group if I would start singing with the choir at the local Presbyterian Church. So I agreed. Now this was the first time in my life I had sung in a Church Choir and it was a fine experience. We practiced one night a week and briefly before the 11 AM service on Sundays. Our conductor was Mary-Lou Norris, a very talented and beautiful lady. She had lots of ideas and our choir was always doing a lot of original things. We lived in DeBordieu for ten years and I sang in the choir all of that time. There was no getting away from it, my golf career had come full circle and so had my singing and music interests.

All of this singing aroused some latent interest in me to start writing some music. I did some individual songs and then put together an entire Christmas Album, which we recorded with the DeBordieu singers in the late nineties. I also joined the American Society of Composers and Publishers. ASCAP as it is known. My songs have been well received and some have also been recorded by other artists but the big problem in promoting your own music is that you need to be performing regularly and as a Super Senior I was not about to start another singing career.

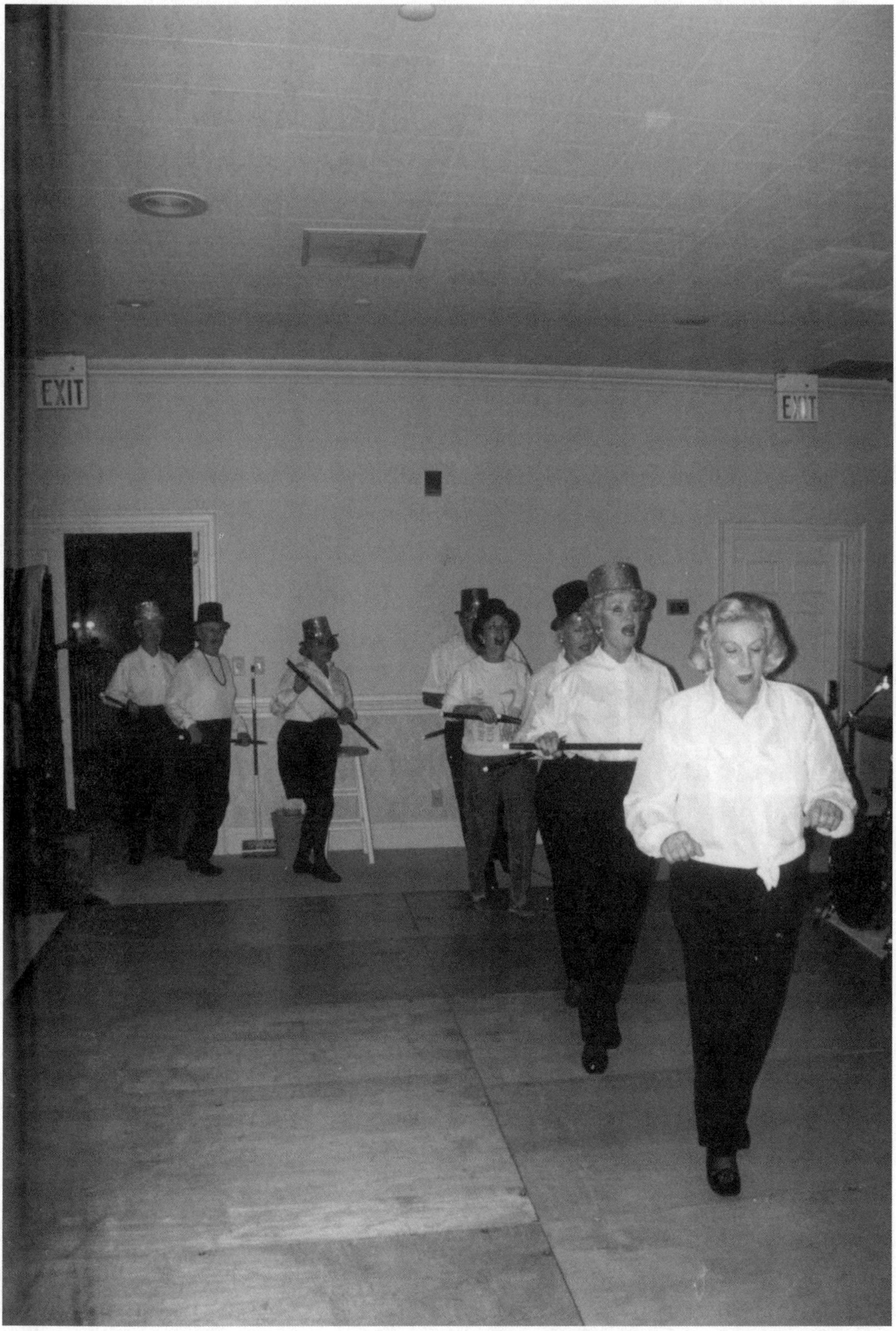
EXIT

Next thing up was putting on a show at DeBordieu with the singers and other members I recruited. We had a cast of forty. I started a tap dancing group and the first show we did was an enormous success. I wrote, directed and produced the show and before I knew it we were planning our second show. It was so much fun! This show was all about the chorus flying down to Rio and trying to find Elvis Presley. When we got to Rio, we contacted the local Sheriff and his staff, and in the following years, those members were known as the Sheriff and the Sheriff's wife, etc. You have no idea how much work and rehearsing this all took. We had rented a spotlight and sound system and Werner ran the spotlight for our shows. John Abernethy, our golf Pro, had a good sized skit with our Tennis Pro who spoke French, so we utilized everyone's talents. I really could have done another show, but time marched on and we soon moved to Belfair Golf Club and this club did not have a ballroom where we could stage such a show. Oh well, I guess enough is enough. We have a singing group here and we do a couple of events a year.

Possibly our most well known members at DeBordieu were Governor Carroll Campbell and his great wife Iris. They were avid and good golfers. One day Iris played with me on an interclub team event at Pawley's Island. We had a grand time and later one of our foursome complained to me how she was distracted by the Secret Service guard who was assigned to Iris. He walked along in the rough and never bothered anyone.

One Christmas we were invited along with three or four other couples to the Governor's Mansion in Columbia. I took my camera and no one else did. I asked if it was okay to take pictures and then of course everyone else wanted their picture taken.

In 1988 we went on a Crystal Cruise with six other couples from DeBordieu from San Francisco to Vancouver and on to Alaska. The Cruise was about sixteen days and simply wonderful. When we docked in Vancouver I had a chance to visit some old friends and tour around the city. In some ways it hadn't changed a lot and in other ways it had. Still an outstanding city in anyone's book. The present Mayor of Vancouver in 2007 is Sam Sullivan. His life's story is amazing. He is a paraplegic as a result of a bad skiing accident in 1979. I was very inspired when I read his story in Guidepost magazine. He is an inspiration.

Again, I received an invitation to go to Connecticut and be present for the 25th Anniversary of the Longshore Golf Club. We did that and I enjoyed meeting up again with my long time friend, Mimi Levitt of New York, who has a summer home in Westport. What a treat to spend some time with old friends, and we also have stayed in touch. Mimi's late husband Mortimer Levitt was the founder of the Levitt Pavilions of which there are several, but the one most known to me is the Levitt Pavilion in Westport, CT. Like the Malkin Bowl in Vancouver and the Hollywood Bowl in California, these huge concert areas promote the best in entertainment.

In 1999, we completed building a new home in Belfair, on the mainland off of Hilton Head Island. A great plantation with two top-notch golf courses and a most outstanding learning center. Our teaching Pro is Krista Dunton, and she is the 2007 golf teacher of the year for the Southeast section of the LPGA. Our fine golf staff is directed by Bill Anderson and his assistants, Hugh, Shane, and Doug.

We have traveled a great deal and have gone on a few great cruises with friends and family. Three times I have sung with the band on a cruise and we all got a big kick out of that. We have many fine friends here and I'm pretty sure that we are settled down.

We celebrated our twenty-fifth Wedding Anniversary, September 17, 2002 at the Evergreen Inn and Golf Club in Rangeley, Maine. This club is owned by my son George. It is a beautiful place and the golf course is now five years old. A Mountain course, designed and built by George. Our party was terrific and we had forty guests, including seven couples from Belfair. It was a Lobster & Champagne dinner at the Inn and we also played golf and had dinner at two or three other places in the area. We had hoped to have Goldie Hawn and Kurt Russell as guests, but they couldn't come. Kurt grew up and went to school in Rangeley. His parents, Bing and Louise had moved to California, but came back to Rangeley every summer. You could write a book about Bing and his boys. Bing and Louise came to our party and had a grand time. Very sadly, it was the last year that we saw them as Bing passed on in 2003.

Rangeley is the location of the Saddleback Mountain Ski Resort which has recently been developed into a major ski area. Rangeley is also known as the Snowmobile resort of the World! So it is indeed a very busy location in Maine.

The saddest event in my life happened in December of 2004 when my younger son Gary died of injuries from a bad car accident. We never thought he wouldn't make it, but after thirteen days in intensive care in Charleston, he passed on. A part of me died too that day and I guess anyone who has had such an ordeal will know what I mean. Gary was a fine musician and just a good, smart, and loving person. Both of my sons have been a joy to me. Both good musicians professionally and top-notch golfers, too. They say the apple doesn't fall far from the tree. Every day I think of Gary and I am very aware of his presence. Werner's three children and their families are a continuous pleasure to us and they all live in the West.

DeBORDIEU 1996

I have had a lot of loves in my life. Many careers and events that have been thoroughly enjoyable. Many good friends from all walks of life. And my family that has always brought me such rewards. The tapestries of my life that continued to form along the way have designed a richness I could never improve upon. We live in a community of wonderful people. Avid golfers, tennis players and theatre goers. No one could ever have asked for more.

Live, Love and Laugh. Swinging and Singing, My Way.

GOLF DIGEST
THE GOLF COMPANY®

Age Shooter Certificate
awarded by
GOLF DIGEST MAGAZINE

to *Beryl Buck Miller*

on *October 23, 1996*, at age *75*, who played the *DeBordieu Golf Club* course in *75* strokes.

Jerry Tarde
Jerry Tarde, Vice President & Editor

A New York Times Company

Patty Berg
P. O. BOX 9227
FORT MYERS, FLA. 33902

February 3, 1998

Ms. Beryl Buck Miller
1594 Wallace Pate Dr.
Georgetown, SC 29440

Dear Beryl:

    A quick note on a not-so-slow morning to thank you not only for your lovely Christmas card, but also for the tape of you and the DeBordieu Singers. Listening to the tape took me back to when, as a girl, I along with my childhood friends sang - happily - the songs of Christmas. It was always a magic time, and you and your singers helped me recall it.
    I'm impressed by your talents not only as a singer, but as a songwriter as well. I thought your contributions were outstanding, so much so they should become seasonal standards. With a little luck, maybe?
    I'm well, happy to say, and I have a busy year ahead, which you can bet pleases me, especially in that I'm roaring toward my 80th birthday (Feb. 13). The Unsinkable Molly Brown had nothing on me.
    Again, Beryl, thanks for thinking of me.

Cordially,

Patty

Patty J Berg

Celeste, Werner, Beryl - January 2007 - Panama Canal Trip

Celeste Simon
Boynton Beach, Florida
April, 2007

Shortly after I arrived in New York City to pursue a career in theater and music, I was given two very special gifts. I met Jerry Simon, whom I married in 1982, and I met beautiful Beryl (Buck) Miller.

When I was first introduced to Jerry, I was told that he was a "bit of a legend". He had been a successful publicist, music producer and president of his record company R.S.V.P. Records. Under the aegis of his R.S.V.P. record label, he was the first to record Jimi Hendrix as a solo artist.

On my first date with Jerry, which took place at the New York Friars Club in Manhattan, I met another legendary being, Beryl (Buck) Miller. Jerry informed me that Beryl had been a very successful singer on radio and television and was now a professional lady golf pro. So, I was really a little overwhelmed at meeting such a lovely, sophisticated, accomplished lady - which lasted all of five minutes! Beryl with her usual grace and warmth immediately put me at ease.

Jerry told me then, and many times over the years, that Beryl was the "sister of his heart". And so it was. And so it continued. I was the beneficiary of their relationship, because I became part of their "family". Fortunately, Beryl and I have been able to maintain our close connection, and it has deepened across the years. It is something I truly cherish.

As my life days have passed by, I have learned the truth of love through my relationship with Jerry and his final journey with Alzheimer's Disease – and through my ever enduring friendship with Beryl.

Currently, I am the Administrative Director for the World Affairs Council of the Florida Palm Beaches. In addition, I continue to sing professionally, and ,like Beryl, I continue to share my joy of music with all.

Celeste Simon

Alaska Glaciers

Christmas Party at the Governor's Mansion - Columbia, SC

Barbershop Quartet - Beryl's 85th Surprise Birthday Party